Practical Ideas
That Really Work
for Students with Autism Spectrum Disorders

Second Edition

Kathleen McConnell

Gail R. Ryser

pro·ed
An International Publisher

8700 Shoal Creek Boulevard
Austin, Texas 78757-6897
800/897-3202   Fax 800/397-7633
www.proedinc.com

© 2000, 2007 by PRO-ED, Inc.
8700 Shoal Creek Boulevard
Austin, Texas 78757-6897
800/897-3202   Fax 800/397-7633
www.proedinc.com

ISBN-13: 978-141640227-5
ISBN-10: 1-4164-0227-6

Printed in the United States of America

4   5   6   7   8   9   10   10

Contents

Introduction

Practical Ideas That Really Work for Students with Autism Spectrum Disorders was written to assist educators and parents in providing intervention strategies to promote these students' ability to learn and to function in social situations. The book builds on the feedback that we have collectively received about our prior books in this series. We have learned that teachers find it very useful to have a repertoire of appropriate intervention strategies to use.

Background

Leo Kanner (1943) first introduced the term *early infantile autism*. Kanner used behavioral observation as the basis for describing a group of 11 children who had similar characteristics but who did not fit into diagnostic categories that were typically used at the time. Kanner initially considered both biological and environmental variables and their interaction as possible causes of autism. He felt that children seemed to have been born without the typical capacity for social and emotional development, perhaps due to some organic or neurological problem. It is now accepted that autism is caused by some form of neurological brain abnormality (Rapin, 2001; Schopler & Mesibov, 1995). Regardless of the causes of autism, the increase in prevalence rates will result in increased referrals for special education services and an increased need for educational accommodations.

The prevalence rate for autism was first reported as five cases in 10,000 children by Wing, Yeates, Brierley, and Gould (1976). In recent years, the reported prevalence rate for autism has increased. Fombonne (2003) summarized the results of 32 epidemiological surveys conducted worldwide. He found that between 1966 and 2001 the prevalence rate increased to 12.7 cases in 10,000 children. When he included studies that combined all Pervasive Developmental Disorders, he reported an estimated prevalence rate of 27.5 cases in 10,000 children. Fombonne and others project that the prevalence rate will reach 40 cases in 10,000 children by the year 2050.

This increase in prevalence rates has major implications for educational interventions and accommodations for students with autism spectrum disorders. We have designed these materials to meet these students' needs by using research-based strategies.

Components

Practical Ideas That Really Work for Students with Autism Spectrum Disorders is intended for use with students with autism spectrum disorders in preschool through Grade 12 It includes the following two primary components.

- **Evaluation Form with a Rating Scale and Ideas Matrix.** The Rating Scale portion of the evaluation form is a criterion-referenced measure for evaluating behaviors that impact student learning and social interactions. The items on the scale are specific descriptors that correlate to the *Diagnostic and Statistical Manual of Mental Disorders–Fourth Edition–Text Revision* (DSM–IV–TR; American Psychiatric Association, 2000) indicators for Autistic Disorder. All DSM–IV–TR criteria for Autistic Disorder are included on the scale. Additionally, many of the items apply to other PDDs. On the third page of the Evaluation Form we have included a table that indicates which items relate to each of the other PDDs. The Ideas Matrix on the last page of the Evaluation Form provides a systematic way of linking the results of the Rating Scale to interventions. We hope that educators use the Ideas Matrix as a tool for selecting effective interventions to meet each student's specific needs.

- **Practical Ideas Manual.** The manual was developed to meet the needs of students with a range of pervasive developmental disorders. The ideas in the manual were written to assist teachers and other professionals in improving students' social interactions and communication skills and in decreasing their repetitive and stereotypical patterns of behaviors. The name of the book reflects our understanding that students with these disorders can exhibit a wide spectrum of skills and behaviors related to social interactions, communication, and repetitive/stereotypical behaviors. The book contains an explanation of each idea, along with reproducible worksheets, examples, illustrations, and tips designed for easy implementation. There are also many references to other materials that teachers may find useful.

The Rating Scale

The Rating Scale included within the Evaluation Form is a criterion-referenced instrument. It was designed to be used by teachers or other professionals to rate children and adolescents according to the DSM–IV–TR criteria for autism and other PDDs. The measure was designed to assist teachers in conducting a careful and thorough assessment of the specific problems to guide the selection of intervention strategies. This scale is not intended to be used to diagnose these disorders, rather it is intended as a tool for determining intervention strategies and writing Individualized Education Program (IEP) goals and objectives.

Item Development

The Rating Scale is divided into the three areas of Autistic Disorder defined by the DSM–IV–TR: Social Interactions, Communication, and Repetitive/Stereotyped Patterns. The measure consists of 39 items; three items for each of the 12 DSM–IV–TR criteria and three for receptive language, for a total of 13 criteria. Professionals are to answer the following question when rating a student: To what degree do the behaviors listed interfere with the student's ability to function in the learning or social environments? The items on the scale are to be rated by educators using the 4-point Likert system with 0 = *Never or rarely exhibits the behavior,* 1 = *Sometimes exhibits the behavior,* 2 = *Frequently exhibits the behavior,* and 3 = *Consistently exhibits the behavior.* For each criterion, the range of possible scores is 0 to 9; the higher the score, the more the behavior interferes with the student's ability to function in the learning and social environments.

Field-Testing the Rating Scale

The criterion-referenced measure was field-tested in four school districts in Texas with 50 students identified as having autism. The students ranged in age from 3 to 18 years; 12 were females and 38 were males. An item analysis was conducted using this sample, and the resulting reliability coefficients were .91 for social interactions, .90 for communication, and .92 for repetitive/stereotyped behaviors. The magnitude of these coefficients strongly suggests that the rating scale possesses little test error and that users can have confidence in its results.

The Manual

Teachers and other educators are busy people who have many responsibilities. In our discussions with teachers, supervisors, and counselors about the development of this product, they consistently emphasized the need for materials that are practical, easy to implement in the classroom, and not overly time-consuming. We appreciated their input and worked hard to meet their criteria as we developed the ideas in this book. In addition, we conducted an extensive review of the literature, so that we stayed focused on ideas supported by data documenting their effectiveness. The result is a book with 40 ideas, many with reproducible masters, and all grounded in research and the collective experience of the many educators who advised us and shared information with us.

Assessment provides useful information to educators about the strengths and deficits of students. However, unless the information gathered during the assessment process impacts instruction, its usefulness for campus-based educators is limited. We designed the Ideas Matrix so that educators can make the direct link between the information provided by the Rating Scale and instruction in the classroom. We think that this format stays true to our purpose of presenting information that is practical and useful.

Directions for Using the Materials

Step 1: Collect Student Information

The professional (a special education teacher, general education teacher, counselor, or other educator with knowledge of the student) should begin by completing the Evaluation Form for the child who has been identified as having autism or another pervasive developmental disorder. In addition, the professional can use this product with children who exhibit problems functioning in the learning or social environment because of poor social interactions or communication skills, or who exhibit repetitive or stereotypical patterns of behaviors.

As an example, Torrance's completed Evaluation Form is provided in Figure 1. Space is provided on the front of the form for pertinent information about the student being rated, including name, birth date, age, school, grade, rater, and educational setting. In addition, the dates the student is observed and the amount of time the rater spends with the student can be recorded. Also included on the front of the form are the DSM–IV–TR criteria for Autistic Disorder.

Step 2: Rate the Behaviors of the Student

Pages 2 and 3 of the Evaluation Form contain the Rating Scale. The items are divided into the three sections defined by the DSM–IV–TR criteria for autistic disorder: social interactions, communication, and repetitive/stereotypical patterns. This section provides the instructions for administering and scoring the items. Space is also provided to total the items for each DSM–IV–TR criterion, to check the three problems to target for immediate intervention and to record the intervention idea and its starting date. At the bottom of the rating scale is a table that depicts which items of the rating scale are aligned to the DSM–IV–TR criteria for four disorders: Autistic Disorder, Asperger's Disorder, Childhood Disintegrative Disorder, and Rett's Disorder.

Step 3: Choose the Ideas To Implement

The last page of the Evaluation Form contains the Ideas Matrix. After choosing the three priority problems to target for immediate intervention, the professional should turn to the Ideas Matrix and select an intervention that corresponds to that problem. The professional should write the idea number and the starting date on the space provided on the rating scale.

For example, Torrance received the highest ratings in one area of Reptetive/Stereotyped Patterns (restricted patterns of interest [9]) and one area of Communication (conversation [7]) and one area of Social Interactions (sharing enjoyment and interests [6]). His teacher has targeted these three areas and has chosen Ideas 3, 16, 27, and 29 from the Ideas Matrix. Because the area of major concern is restricted patterns of interest, the teacher will begin with Ideas 27 and 29 on September 10.

Step 4: Read and Review the Practical Ideas That Have Been Selected

Within the manual, the ideas are discussed at some length in terms of their intent and implementation. After selecting the idea that is matched to the needs of students, the idea can then be planned for implementation. These individual ideas should be integrated into an overall instructional design and be reflected in one or several classroom lessons focused on the particular learning objective.

In our example with Torrance, this could be accomplished by recording the number of times he completes or demonstrates the targeted action or behavior independently during a 6- to 8-week period. The teacher can either move on to the second problem at this point or work on more than one problem simultaneously. In the case of Torrance, the teacher plans to use Idea 3, Show Me, to improve his ability to share his enjoyment and Idea 16, Cueing Pronouns, to improve his ability to use the appropriate pronoun when engaged in conversation.

Step 5: Evaluation

After implementation, teachers should complete the assessment cycle by evaluating the results of the intervention strategy. By following a model that begins with the assessment of need, leads to the development of an instructional plan, follows with the implementation plan, and concludes with the evaluation of its effectiveness, teachers can ensure a responsive educational program that enables students to enhance their achievement in the area of concern. In so doing, the information within this manual can be correlated with the annual goal-setting of students with autism spectrum disorders.

References

American Psychiatric Association. (2000). *Diagnostic and statistical manual of mental disorders–Fourth edition–Text revision*. Washington, DC: Author.

Fombonne, E. (2003). Epidemiological surveys of autism and other pervasive developmental disorders: An update. *Journal of Autism and Developmental Disorders, 33*, 365–382.

Kanner, L. (1943). Autistic disturbances of affective content. *The Nervous Child, 2*, 217–250.

Rapin, I. (2001). *Autistic children: Diagnosis and clinical features*. Elk Grove, IL: American Academy of Pediatrics.

Schopler, E., & Mesibov, G. B. (1995). Introduction to learning and cognition in autism. In E. Schopler & G. B. Mesibov (Eds.), *Learning and cognition in autism* (pp. 3–11). New York: Plenum Press.

Wing, L., Yeates, S., Brierley, L. M., & Gould, J. (1976). The prevalence of early childhood autism: A comparison of administrative and epidemiological studies. *Psychological Medicine, 6*, 89–100.

References Supporting Ideas

1. Adams, C., Lloyd, J., Aldred, C., & Baxendale, J. (2006). Exploring effects of communication intervention for developmental pragmatic language impairments: A signal-generation study. *International Journal of Language and Communication Disorders, 41*(1), 41–65.
   Ideas 6, 11, 14, 18, 19, 20, 21

2. Adams, L., Gouvousis, A., VanLue, M., & Waldron, C. (2004). Social story intervention: Improving communication skills in a child with autism spectrum disorder. *Focus on Autism and Other Developmental Disabilities, 19*(2), 87–94.
   Idea 34

3. Apple, A. L., Billingsley, F., & Schwartz, I. S. (2005). Effects of video modeling alone and with self-management on compliment-giving behaviors of children with high-functioning ASD. *Journal of Positive Behavior Interventions, 7*(1), 33–46.
Ideas 9, 35

4. Baker, M. J. (2000). Incorporating the thematic ritualistic behaviors of children with autism into games: Increasing social play interactions with siblings. *Journal of Positive Behavior Interventions, 2*(2), 66–84.
Ideas 8, 13

5. Barrows, P. (2004). "Playful" therapy: Working with autism and trauma. *International Forum Psychoanalysis, 13,* 175–186
Idea 13

6. Barry, L. M., & Burlew, S. B. (2004). Using social stories to teach choice and play skills to children with autism. *Focus on Autism and Other Developmental Disabilities, 19*(1), 45–51.
Idea 34

7. Bauminger, N. (2002). The facilitation of social-emotional understanding and social interaction in high-functioning children with autism: Intervention outcomes. *Journal of Autism and Developmental Disorders, 32*(4), 283–298.
Ideas 3, 39

8. Bryan, L. C., & Gast, D. L. (2000). Teaching on-task and on-schedule behaviors to high-functioning children with autism via picture activity schedules. *Journal of Autism and Developmental Disorders, 30*(6), 553–567.
Ideas 12, 24, 25, 28

9. Carothers, D. E., & Taylor, R. L. (2004). How teachers and parents can work together to teach daily living skills to children with autism. *Focus on Autism & Other Developmental Disabilities, 19*(2), 102–104.
Idea 22

10. Christodulu, K. V., & Durand, V. M. (2004). Reducing bedtime disturbance and night waking using positive bedtime routines and sleep restriction. *Focus on Autism and Other Developmental Disabilities, 19*(3), 130–139.
Idea 27

11. Conroy, M. A., Asmus, J. M., Sellers, J. A., & Ladwig, C. N. (2005). The use of an antecedent-based intervention to decrease stereotypic behavior in a general education classroom: A case study. *Focus on Autism and Other Developmental Disabilities, 20*(4), 223–230.
Ideas 2, 28, 29, 32

12. Dauphin, M., Kinney, E. M., & Stromer, R. (2004). Using video-enhanced activity schedules and matrix training to teach sociodramatic play to a child with autism. *Journal of Positive Behavior Interventions, 6*(4), 238–250.
Ideas 9, 25, 35

13. Dettmer, S., Simpson, R. L., Myles, B. S., & Ganz, J. B. (2000). The use of visual supports to facilitate transitions of students with autism. *Focus on Autism and Other Developmental Disabilities, 15*(3), 163–169.
Ideas 24, 25, 26, 28, 29, 30, 32, 33

14. Diehl, S. F., Ford, C. S., & Federico, J. (2005). The communication journey of a fully included child with an autism spectrum disorder. *Topics in Language Disorders, 25*(4), 375–387.
Ideas 12, 18, 22, 23, 27, 34

15. Dyer, K., Dunlap, G., & Winterling, V. (1990). Effects of choice making on the serious problem behaviors of students with severe handicaps. *Journal of Applied Behavior Analysis, 23,* 515–524.
Ideas 23, 24

16. Earles, T. L., Carlson, J. K., & Bock, S. J. (1998). Instructional strategies to facilitate successful learning outcomes for students with autism. In R. L. Simpson & B. S. Myles (Eds.), *Educating children and youth with autism: Strategies for effective practice* (pp. 55–111). Austin, TX: PRO-ED.
Ideas 12, 24, 25

17. Escalona, A., Field, T., Nadel, J., & Lundy, B. (2002). Brief report: Imitation effects on children with autism. *Journal of Autism & Developmental Disorders, 32*(2), 141–144.
Ideas 4, 5

18. Field, T., Field, T., Sanders, C., & Nadel, J. (2001). Children with autism display more social behaviors after repeated imitation sessions. *Autism: The International Journal of Research & Practice, 5*(3), 317–323.
Ideas 5, 11

19. Fisher, W., Adelinis, J. D., Volkert, V. M., Keeney, K. M., Neidart, P. L., & Hovanetz, A. (2005). Assessing preferences for positive and negative reinforcement during treatment of destructive behavior with functional communication training. *Research in Developmental Disabilties, 26*(2), 153–168.
Ideas 36, 37

20. Heflin, L. J., & Alberto, P. (2001). Establishing a behavioral context for learning for students with autism. *Focus on Autism and Other Developmental Disabilities, 69*(2), 93–101.
Ideas 17, 30, 38, 39, 40

21. Hess, L. (2006). I would like to play but I don't know how: A case study of pretend play in autism. *Child Language Teaching and Therapy, 22*(1), 97–116.
Idea 39

22. Ingersoll, B., Dvortcsak, A., Whalen, C., & Sikora, D. (2005). The effects of a developmental, social-pragmatic language intervention on rate of expressive language production in young children with autistic spectrum disorders. *Focus on Autism and Other Developmental Disabilities, 20*(4), 231–222.
Ideas 5, 11, 14, 17, 18, 19, 20

23. Ingersoll, B., Schreibman, L., & Tran, Q. H. (2003). Effect of sensory feedback on immediate object imitation in children with autism. *Journal of Autism & Developmental Disorders, 33*(6), 673–683.
Idea 4, 5, 10

24. Ivey, M. L., Heflin, L. J., & Alberto, P. (2004). The use of social stories to promote independent behaviors in novel events for children with PDD–NOS. *Focus on Autism and Other Developmental Disabilities, 19*(3), 164–176.
Idea 34

25. Kay, S., Harchik, A. E., & Luiselli, J. K. (2006). Elimination of drooling by an adolescent student with autism attending public high school. *Journal of Positive Behavior Interventions, 8*(1), 24–28.
Ideas 36, 37

26. Keen, D., Sigafoos, J., & Woodyatt, G. (2001). Replacing prelinguistic behaviors with functional communication. *Journal of Autism and Developmental Disorders, 31*(4), 385–398.
Ideas 6, 17, 23

27. Kerr, S., & Durkin, K. (2004). Understanding of thought bubbles as mental representations in children with autism: Implications for theory of mind. *Journal of Autism and Developmental Disorders, 34*(6), 637–648.
Idea 21

28. Koegel, L. K., Camarata, S. M., & Valdez-Menchaca, M. C. (1998). Setting generalization of question-asking by children with autism. *American Journal on Mental Retardation, 102,* 346–357.
Idea 17

29. Kok, A. J., Kong, T. Y., & Bernard-Opitz, V. (2002). A comparison of the effects of structured play and facilitated play approaches on preschoolers with autism. *Autism: The International Journal of Research & Practice, 6*(2), 181–196.
Ideas 6, 7, 8, 13

30. LeBlanc, L. A., Coates, A. M., Daneshvar, S., Charlop-Christy, M. H., Morris, C., & Lancaster, B. M. (2003). Using video modeling and reinforcement to teach perspective-taking skills to children with autism. *Journal of Applied Behavior Analysis, 36*(2), 253–257.
Ideas 9, 35

31. McDuff, G. S., Krantz, P. J., & McClannahan, L. E. (1993). Teaching children with autism to use photographic activity schedules: Maintenance and generalization of complex response chains. *Journal of Applied Behavior Analysis, 26,* 89–97.
Ideas 12, 25, 26

32. McDuffie, A., Yoder, P., & Stone, W. (2005). Prelinguistic predictors of vocabulary in young children with autism spectrum disorders. *Journal of Speech, Language, & Hearing Research, 48*(5), 1080–1097.
Idea 4

33. McGee, G. G., Daly, T., Izeman, S. G., Man, L., & Risley, T. R. (1991). Use of classroom materials to promote preschool engagement. *Teaching Exceptional Children, 23,* 44–47.
Idea 30

34. Olley, J. G. (1999). Curriculum for students with autism. *School Psychology Review, 28*(4), 595–607.
Ideas 17, 38, 39, 40

35. Quill, K. (1997). Instructional considerations for young children with autism: The rationale for visually cued instruction. *Journal of Autism and Developmental Disorders, 27*(6), 697–714.
Ideas 1, 2, 12, 15, 16, 32, 33

36. Ruff, H. A., & Saltarelli, L. M. (1993). Exploratory play with objects: Basic cognitive processes and individual differences. In M. H. Bornstein & A. W. O'Reilly (Eds.), *The role of play in the development of thought* (pp. 5–16). San Francisco: Jossey-Bass.
Idea 10

37. Schaff, R. C., & Miller, L. J. (2005). Occupational therapy using a sensory integrative approach for children with developmental disorders. *Mental Retardation and Developmental Disabilities Research Reviews, 11,* 143–148.
Idea 10

38. Schepis, M. M., Reid, D. H., Behrmann, M. M., & Sutton, K. A. (1998). Increasing communicative interactions of young children with autism using a voice output communication aid and naturalistic teaching. *Journal of Applied Learning Analysis, 31,* 561–578.
Ideas 1, 15

39. Schwartz, I. S., Sandall, S. R., McBride, B. J., & Boulware, G. L. (2004). Project DATA (developmentally appropriate treatment for autism): An inclusive school-based approach to educating young children with autism. *Topics in Early Childhood Special Education, 24*(3), 156–168.
Ideas 21, 23, 24, 27, 33, 36, 37

40. Shabini, D. B., Katz, R. C., Wilder, D. A., Beauchamp, K., Taylor, C. R., & Fischer, K. J. (2002). Increasing social initiations in children with autism: Effects of a tactile prompt. *Journal of Applied Behavior Analysis, 35*(1), 79–83.
Idea 31

41. Sherratt, D. (2002). Developing pretend play in children with autism: A case study. *Autism: The International Journal of Research & Practice, 6*(2), 169–171.
Ideas 13, 35

42. Shields, J. (2001). The NAS EarlyBird Programme. *Autism: The International Journal of Research & Practice, 5*(1), 49–56.
Idea 22

43. Simpson, R. L., & Myles, B. S. (1998). Understanding and responding to the needs of students with autism. In R. L. Simpson & B. S. Myles (Eds.), *Educating children and youth with autism: Strategies for effective practice* (pp. 1–23). Austin, TX: PRO-ED.
Idea 25

44. Solomon, M., Goodlin-Jones, B. L., & Anders, T. F. (2004). A social adjustment enhancement intervention for high functioning autism, Asperger's syndrome, and pervasive developmental disorders NOS. *Journal of Autism and Developmental Disorders, 34*(6), 649–668.
Idea 3

45. Soorya, L. V., Arnstein, L. M., Gillis, J., & Romanczyk, R. G. (2003). An overview of imitation skills in autism: Implications for practice. *The Behavior Analyst Today, 4*(2), 114–123.
Idea 4

46. Tabor, T. A., Seltzer, A., Heflin, L. J., & Alberto, P. A. (1999). Use of self-operated auditory prompts to decrease off-task behavior for a student with autism and moderate mental retardation. *Focus on Autism and Other Developmental Disabilities, 14*(3), 159–166.
Ideas 31

47. Tissot, C., & Evans, R. (2003). Visual teaching strategies for children with autism. *Early Child Development and Care, 173*(4), 425–433.
Ideas 2, 15, 16, 32

48. Whitaker, P. (2004). Fostering communication and shared play between mainstream peers and children with autism: Approaches, outcomes and experiences. *British Journal of Special Education, 31*(4), 215–222.
Ideas 7, 8, 13

49. Woods, J., & Goldstein, H. (2003). When the toddler takes over: Changing challenging routines into conduits for communication. *Focus on Autism and Other Developmental Disabilities, 18*(3), 176–181.
Idea 27

Ideas	Supporting References
1 Show You Know	35, 38
2 Nice Looking	11, 35, 47
3 Show Me	7, 44
4 Learn To Imitate, Imitate To Learn	17, 23, 32, 45
5 Your Turn To Imitate	17, 18, 22, 23
6 Your Turn, My Turn	1, 26, 29
7 Follow the Music	29, 48
8 Games, Games, and More Games	4, 29, 48
9 Look in the Mirror	3, 12, 30
10 Schedule Sensory Time	22, 23, 36, 37
11 Bring Out the Noise	1, 18, 22
12 When/Do Books	8, 14, 16, 31, 35
13 Puppet Play	4, 5, 29, 41, 48
14 Get Predictable	1, 22
15 Yes or No	35, 38, 47
16 Cueing Pronouns	35, 47
17 Touch, Show, Find, or Say	20, 22, 26, 28, 34
18 Wh– Game	1, 14, 22
19 Talk Prompters	1, 22
20 Conversation Cards	1, 22
21 Problem Solve with I Think, You Think	1, 27, 39
22 The Daily Scoop	9, 14, 42
23 Choice Cards	14, 15, 26, 39
24 Now–Next Picture Map	8, 13, 15, 16, 39
25 Schedule Changes	8, 12, 13, 16, 31, 43
26 Learn To Wait	13, 31
27 Teaching Independence	10, 14, 39, 49
28 Do More To Learn More	8, 11, 13
29 On Your Own	11, 13
30 Five Ways To Finish	13, 20, 33
31 Reduce Prompts	40, 46
32 Door Signs	11, 13, 35, 47
33 Four-Step Behavior Plan	13, 35, 39
34 Social Skills in Pictures	2, 6, 14, 24
35 Use Video Modeling	3, 12, 30, 41
36 Card Counters	19, 25, 39
37 Positive Reinforcement	19, 25, 39
38 What To Teach Next	20, 34
39 Direct-Teach Social Skills	7, 20, 21, 34
40 Skills Checklists	20, 34

Practical Ideas
That Really Work
for Students with Autism Spectrum Disorders

Second Edition

Kathleen McConnell • Gail R. Ryser

Evaluation Form

Name Torrance Wilson

Birth Date April 12, 1997   **Age** 9

School Carver Elementary   **Grade** 3

Rater Ms. Martinez (teacher)

Educational Setting self-contained classroom

Dates Student Observed: From Aug. 15 **To** Sept. 4

Amount of Time Spent with Student:

Per Day 4 hrs.   **Per Week** 20 hrs.

DSM–IV–TR Diagnostic Criteria for Autistic Disorder

A. A total of six (or more) items from (1), (2), and (3), with at least two from (1), and one each from (2) and (3):

(1) qualitative impairment in social interaction, as manifested by at least two of the following:

  (a) marked impairment in the use of multiple nonverbal behaviors such as eye-to-eye gaze, facial expression, body postures, and gestures to regulate social interaction

  (b) failure to develop peer relationships appropriate to developmental level

  (c) a lack of spontaneous seeking to share enjoyment, interests, or achievements with other people (e.g., by a lack of showing, bringing, or pointing out objects of interest)

  (d) lack of social or emotional reciprocity

(2) qualitative impairments in communication as manifested by at least one of the following:

  (a) delay in, or total lack of , the development of spoken language (not accompanied by an attempt to compensate through alternative modes of communication such as gesture or mime)

  (b) in individuals with adequate speech, marked impairment in the ability to initiate or sustain a conversation with others

  (c) stereotyped and repetitive use of language or idiosyncratic language

  (d) lack of varied, spontaneous make-believe play or social imitative play appropriate to developmental level

(3) restricted repetitive and stereotyped patterns of behavior, interests, and activities, as manifested by at least one of the following:

  (a) encompassing preoccupation with one or more stereotyped and restricted patterns of interest that is abnormal either in intensity or focus

  (b) apparently inflexible adherence to specific, nonfunctional routines or rituals

  (c) stereotyped and repetitive motor mannerisms (e.g., hand or finger flapping or twisting, or complex whole-body movements)

  (d) persistent preoccupation with parts of objects

B. Delays or abnormal functioning in at least one of the following areas, with onset prior to age 3 years: (1) social interaction, (2) language as used in social communication, or (3) symbolic or imaginative play.

C. The disturbance is not better accounted for by Rett's Disorder or Childhood Disintegrative Disorder.

Note. From the *Diagnostic and Statistical Manual of Mental Disorders–Fourth Edition–Text Revision* (p. 75), 2000, Washington, DC: American Psychiatric Association. Copyright 2000 by American Psychiatric Association. Reprinted with permission.

Figure 1. Sample Evaluation Form, filled out for Torrance.

(continues)

Rating Scale

DIRECTIONS

❶ Use the following scale to circle the appropriate number:

    0 = *Never or rarely exhibits the behavior*

    1 = *Sometimes exhibits the behavior*

    2 = *Frequently exhibits the behavior*

    3 = *Consistently exhibits the behavior*

❷ Total the ratings and record in the Total box.

❸ Put a checkmark in the Immediate Intervention column by the areas with the lowest scores.

❹ For each area checked, select up to three ideas from the Ideas Matrix on page 4. Write the idea number and start date for each idea in the blanks provided in the last column.

BEHAVIOR	RATING	TOTAL	IMMEDIATE INTERVENTION	IDEA NUMBER; START DATE

Social Interactions

Nonverbal Behaviors

1 Avoids making eye contact or appears to be looking through other people   0 1 ② 3

2 Does not communicate emotions or interest through facial expressions   0 ① 2 3   **5**   ◯   ___ _____

3 Reacts negatively to physical contact (e.g., acts fearful or is totally passive)   0 1 ② 3

Peer Relationships

1 Does not react to the presence of peers   0 ① 2 3

2 Does not initiate relationships with peers   0 1 ② 3   **5**   ◯   ___ _____

3 Does not build or maintain friendships   0 1 ② 3

Sharing Enjoyment and Interests

1 Does not show accomplishments to others   0 1 ② 3

2 Shows little interest in everyday events   0 1 ② 3   **6**   ✓   *3*   *Oct. 1*

3 Does not share enjoyment about an object or activity   0 1 ② 3

Social Reciprocity

1 Does not kiss, hug, or shake hands with others   0 1 ② 3

2 Does not take turns when playing simple games with others   0 ① 2 3   **5**   ◯   ___ _____

3 Prefers to be alone   0 1 ② 3

Communication

Expressive Language

1 Does not speak spontaneously to others   0 ① 2 3

2 Does not use gestures or signs to communicate with others   0 ① 2 3   **4**   ◯   ___ _____

3 Does not let others know through words or gestures his or her needs or desires   0 1 ② 3

Conversation (Rate only if student has spoken language)

1 Does not initiate conversations with others   0 1 ② 3   *16*   *Oct. 1*

2 Fails to use greetings (e.g., hello) or courteous phrases (e.g., please, thank you)   0 1 2 ③   **7**   ✓   ___ _____

3 Does not ask others' questions   0 1 ② 3

Stereotyped Language (Rate only if student has spoken language)

1 Echolalic (i.e., repeats what he or she hears rather than responds appropriately)   0 ① 2 3

2 Perseverates (i.e., repeats the same phrase over and over)   ⓪ 1 2 3   **2**   ◯   ___ _____

3 Recites common phrases heard on television or radio   0 ① 2 3

Figure 1. Continued.

BEHAVIOR	RATING				TOTAL	IMMEDIATE INTERVENTION	IDEA NUMBER; START DATE
	Never/Rarely	Sometimes	Frequently	Consistently			

Make-Believe Play

1 Does not engage in make-believe play appropriate for his or her developmental level	0	①	2	3			
2 Does not join others in play	0	①	2	3	**4**	◯	___ ___
3 Remains aloof or apart from peers	0	1	②	3			___ ___

Receptive Language

1 Does not point to body parts or common objects when asked	0	①	2	3			___ ___
2 Does not respond when spoken to	0	①	2	3	**3**	◯	___ ___
3 Does not respond to simple requests or directions	0	①	2	3			___ ___

Repetitive/Stereotyped Patterns

Restricted Patterns of Interest

1 Prefers to do the same activity over and over	0	1	2	③			27 Sept. 10
2 Becomes upset if preferred activities are interrupted	0	1	2	③	**9**	✓	29 Sept. 10
3 Resists being redirected to other interests	0	1	2	③			___ ___

Nonfunctional Routines or Rituals

1 Engages in unnecessary rituals or routines	0	①	2	3			___ ___
2 Becomes upset if unable to engage in unnecessary rituals or routines	0	1	②	3	**5**	◯	___ ___
3 Resists being redirected to functional activities	0	1	②	3			___ ___

Repetitive Motor Mannerisms

1 Waves fingers in front of face, twirls, etc.	0	①	2	3			___ ___
2 Increases repetitive motor mannerisms when upset	0	1	②	3	**5**	◯	___ ___
3 Resists being redirected to productive behaviors	0	1	②	3			___ ___

Preoccupied with Parts of Objects

1 Intensely scrutinizes parts of objects	0	①	2	3			___ ___
2 Manipulates objects or their parts excessively	⓪	1	2	3	**2**	◯	___ ___
3 Takes toys or other objects apart instead of playing imaginatively with them	0	①	2	3			___ ___

· ·

DSM–IV–TR Criteria for Pervasive Developmental Disorders

This table indicates the criteria for the group of disorders known as pervasive developmental disorders. Use this table to select ideas from the Ideas Matrix for each disorder.

	Nonverbal Behaviors	Peer Relationships	Sharing Enjoyment and Interests	Social Reciprocity	Expressive Language	Conversation	Stereotyped Language	Make-Believe Play	Receptive Language	Restricted Patterns of Interest	Nonfunctional Routines or Rituals	Repetitive Motor Mannerisms	Preoccupied with Parts of Objects
Autistic Disorder	•	•	•	•	•	•	•	•		•	•	•	•
Asperger's Disorder	•	•	•	•						•	•	•	•
Childhood Disintegrative Disorder	•	•		•	•	•	•	•	•	•		•	
Rett's Disorder		•		•	•	•			•				

Figure 1. Continued.

(continues)

Ideas Matrix

Ideas	Social Interactions				Communication					Repetitive Patterns			
	Nonverbal Behaviors	Peer Relationships	Sharing Enjoyment	Social Reciprocity	Expressive Language	Conversation	Stereotyped Language	Make-Believe Play	Receptive Language	Restricted Interests	Nonfunctional Routines	Motor Mannerisms	Preoccupation
1 Show You Know	•	•			•	•			•				
2 Nice Looking	•			•									
3 Show Me	•	•	⊙	•	•				•				
4 Learn To Imitate, Imitate To Learn	•	•	•	•	•	•	•	•	•				
5 Your Turn To Imitate	•	•	•	•	•	•	•	•	•				
6 Your Turn, My Turn	•	•	•	•	•	•	•	•	•				
7 Follow the Music	•	•	•	•	•	•	•	•	•	•	•	•	•
8 Games, Games, and More Games	•	•	•	•	•	•						•	•
9 Look in the Mirror	•		•	•									
10 Schedule Sensory Time	•		•	•				•					
11 Bring Out the Noise		•	•	•	•	•	•						
12 When/Do Books	•	•	•	•	•	•			•				
13 Puppet Play	•	•	•	•	•	•	•	•	•	•		•	•
14 Get Predictable	•	•	•	•	•	•	•		•				
15 Yes or No					•	•	•		•				
16 Cueing Pronouns					•	⊙	•		•				
17 Touch, Show, Find, or Say					•				•				
18 Wh– Game		•	•	•	•	•			•				
19 Talk Prompters	•	•	•	•	•	•	•	•	•	•			
20 Conversation Cards		•	•	•	•	•	•						
21 Problem Solve		•		•	•				•				
22 The Daily Scoop			•	•	•	•			•	•	•		
23 Choice Cards			•		•				•	•	•		
24 Now–Next Picture Map									•	•	•		
25 Schedule Changes									•	•	•	•	
26 Learn To Wait									•	•	•	•	
27 Teaching Independence					•			•	•	⊙	•		
28 Do More To Learn More					•				•	•	•		
29 On Your Own									•	⊙	•		
30 Five Ways To Finish									•	•	•		
31 Reduce Prompts	•	•	•	•	•	•	•	•	•	•	•	•	•
32 Door Signs										•	•		
33 Four-Step Behavior Plan	•	•	•	•	•	•	•	•	•	•	•	•	•
34 Social Skills in Pictures	•	•	•	•	•	•			•	•	•	•	•
35 Use Video Modeling	•	•	•	•	•	•			•	•	•	•	•
36 Card Counters	•	•	•	•	•	•	•	•	•	•	•	•	•
37 Positive Reinforcement	•	•	•	•	•	•			•	•	•	•	•
38 What To Teach Next	•	•	•	•	•	•			•	•	•	•	
39 Direct-Teach Social Skills	•	•	•	•	•	•	•		•	•	•	•	•
40 Skills Checklists	•	•	•	•	•	•	•	•	•	•	•	•	•

Figure 1. Continued.

Idea 1

Show You Know

Communication is the exchange of information and ideas. For communication to be effective, it must be an interactive process that includes both a message sender and a message receiver. Unfortunately, students with autism often do not participate actively in the communication process. Whether it is through body language, gestures, manual signing, pictures, written symbols, sounds, words, or other methods of communication, their skills as both senders and receivers are often limited.

One important communication skill that students with autism may lack is responding to one's name. This skill is so basic that it is a focus of early instruction with young children and may continue even as students grow older. Responding to one's name involves both receiving (hearing the word that is your name and comprehending that it means you) and sending (letting others know that you understand). Although we may think that a student knows his or her name, unless the student responds somehow to indicate this understanding, we cannot be certain. This lack of confirmation may slow or stop the back and forth process of communication.

Here are some ways to teach Show You Know.

❶ With a young child, use a game of Peekaboo. Cover the child's face or hide it behind a scarf, blanket, or other object. Call the child's name and use a question, "Where's ____?" Then remove the cover and point to or touch the child. Repeat, using excitement and prompts to engage the child and reinforce his interest. Tickle and hug whenever possible to encourage the connection between the child's person (his body) and his name. As you play Peekaboo, prompt the child if he is not responding when you call his name, either by touching his cheek, gently turning his head toward you, or placing your face directly in front of his.

② Use a preferred item to gain attention. This is a commonly used strategy that can be adapted for almost any student. When calling the student's name, hold a preferred item in front of the student's face, then move it toward your face, right next to your eyes. Hopefully, the student's gaze will follow the object and she will make eye contact with you each time you say her name. When the eye contact occurs, say her name again and praise her for looking at you.

③ Use a mirror as a teaching tool. Sit next to the student in front of a mirror so that you can both see each other. Say the student's name and touch or point to his face. Repeat this sequence and then begin to prompt the student to turn to you as you say his name. Use a gentle touch on his chin or by the side of his head to help him turn to look at you after you have said his name. Let him check the movement and look in the mirror. Praise him every time he responds when you say his name. Of course, if a student has a pattern of aggression or reacts negatively to touch, use gestures and cues instead of touching him.

④ Teach a verbal response along with a look. Many students with autism have good spoken language, so you will want to teach a student with speech to both look at you and answer when you call her name. Keep the response you teach simple—something like "What?" or "Yes?" As you teach the paired responses, you can use the Show You Know cue card, reminding the student to (a) Look and (b) Say something. Use enthusiastic praise and positive reinforcement each time the student demonstrates both steps.

🦎 Tip:

Consider using Idea 2, Nice Looking, and Idea 16, Cueing Pronouns, with this idea as part of your overall lesson planning. These two related ideas address making eye contact and using personal pronouns to refer to oneself.

Show You Know

When you hear your name,

Look and **Say**

Show You Know

When you hear your name,

Look and **Say**

_____

Idea 1

Idea 2
Nice Looking

Lack of eye contact is one of the defining characteristics of autism spectrum disorders. It is important that students make eye contact with others so that they begin the socialization process and let others know they are paying attention.

To increase eye contact, try these ideas.

❶ As discussed in Idea 1, Show You Know, if you are teaching by direct instruction and are facing the student, hold up a colorful or enticing object right next to your eye. This will encourage the student to move his or her eyes in the right direction.

❷ Consistently use the same verbal direction to request the student to look, regardless of the situation. Throughout the day, whether in the hall, the cafeteria, or at a job site, using the same words will help the student learn to make contact more quickly.

❸ Get excited! Your tone of voice and level of enthusiasm is very important. Use the student's name, say hello, wave, and point to your eyes. Do all you can to focus attention.

❹ For a student who has already learned to make eye contact and just needs to maintain this skill, lots of positive reinforcement after he or she looks at you is the key. Simple, clear comments like "good looking" or "nice eye contact" will help, along with consistent use of the *I Saw Your Eyes* coupons. The coupons can be exchanged for positive reinforcers from a menu.

I Saw Your Eyes

Nice Looking!

I Saw Your Eyes

Nice Looking!

I Saw Your Eyes

Nice Looking!

Idea 2

Idea 3
Show Me

Many students with autism spectrum disorders fail to react with enjoyment, interest, or excitement, even in situations or activities that you know they like. Although it is difficult to teach, showing enthusiasm or interest is an important social skill because it connects students to others, is part of the communication process, and indicates students' awareness of their environment.

One strategy for teaching a student to demonstrate pleasure, interest, enjoyment, or excitement is a two-step procedure involving a prompt then a reinforcer. Our idea has an extra bonus because the prompt itself is part of the reinforcer.

Here's how the plan works.

❶ The first step is to select an object (toy, food, drink), activity (listening to a CD, playing a game, looking at a magazine), or person (Grandma, brother, friend) that you are absolutely certain the student likes a lot. As you introduce the object, activity or person, prompt the student by

- modeling excitement ("Wow, look who's here!");
- gesturing (giving a thumbs up when chocolate ice cream appears); or
- physically prompting (guiding the student's hands to clap for a CD he or she likes).

After the prompt and verbal encouragement to respond ("This is great! Now show me how excited you are by _____."), wait briefly for a response. If the student does not show you an enthusiastic response, repeat the prompt and show the object, activity, or person again.

❷ At the first sign of excitement, follow the second step: reinforce the student immediately by

- giving him or her the object, beginning the preferred activity, or letting the child spend time with his or her favorite person; and
- demonstrating your own enthusiasm by clapping, patting, hugging, praising, or cheering.

In order to maximize chances for success, use reinforcers that are highly valued and preferred by the student. You will know what to pick if you observe the student carefully or let the student create his or her own reinforcement menu.

We have provided forms to accompany this idea. Use the left side of the form in the teaching process to explain how you would like the student to respond and then demonstrate that action. On the right side of the form, write, draw, or place a photo of the student's reinforcer, which can be changed periodically.

Show me a	You will get
 **Smile**	_____

Show me a	You will get
 **Laugh**	_____

Idea 3

Show me a	**You will get**
 Cheer	_____

Show me a	**You will get**
 Clap	_____

Idea 3

Show me a	You will get
![hand waving signal]	
Signal	_____

Show me a	You will get
_____	_____

Idea 3

Idea 4
Learn To Imitate, Imitate To Learn

Imitation is a core skill for students with autism. Through imitation, students can learn important skills without having to be directly taught. Imitation makes learning easier and more efficient. Teaching students with autism spectrum disorders to imitate is a good instructional strategy for teaching fine and gross motor skills and speech. This is especially true for very young children with an autism spectrum disorder, because imitation should be used as a way of learning. The individual behaviors students imitate are sometimes not as important as the cognitive connection they make. For example, the student should think, "Oh, look what he is doing, I can do that too," or "She said this, I'll say it too." The goal is that students not only learn to imitate the actions and language of others in structured teaching situations, but that they also begin to imitate what they see or hear throughout the day.

To teach imitation, it is important to begin with simple physical movements or communicative skills. Once students have learned how to imitate, you can teach more complex behaviors. We have provided a list of basic gross motor imitations and a list of vocalizations and speech imitations to use with students who need to learn to imitate or are very young.

Follow these steps to teach imitation.

❶ Gain the student's attention.

❷ Demonstrate the behavior you want the student to imitate.

❸ Prompt the student to do what you are doing by using gestures, speech, or physical guidance.

❹ Reinforce the student for successful imitations through enthusiastic verbal praise or other reinforcement.

❺ Use the Frequency Chart provided to keep track of which imitations the student has mastered.

✂ Tip:

Once students understand how to imitate, play the statue game. In the statue game, the leader strikes a pose and the players must imitate the leader until a new pose is struck

Here are some imitations to use.

Gross Motor Skills

- Marching (to music or a drum)

- Clapping hands (applause, "Good job")

- Standing up and sitting down (perhaps as a "Simon Says" direction)

- Stomping feet (walk like an elephant)

- Raising arms above one's head (cheering)

- Throwing a kiss (movie star kisses)

- Touching a body part (start with the most obvious first, like the head, tummy, nose, mouth, feet, etc.)

- Jumping or hopping (sometimes on one foot, sometimes with both feet)

- High fives (first with two hands, then one at a time)

- Hugging (everyone's favorite)

Vocalizations and Speech

- Child Vocalizations (imitate sounds the child makes)

- Sounds Depicting Physical Actions (*bye-bye, wheee*)

- Single Syllable Sounds (*shhh, kissing* sound)

- Sounds of Objects (*tick-tock, honk*)

- Animal Sounds (*bark, meow, baaa*)

- Simple Rhymes (Jack and Jill)

Frequency Chart

Student's Name: _____

Write each imitation and prompt level (e.g., gesture, verbal, physical guidance). After each trial, put a slash on a number if the student responds correctly, beginning with the number 1. At the end of five trials, circle the top number that has a slash.

Imitation	Correct Response
	5
	4
_____	3
	2
Prompt Level _____	1
	5
	4
_____	3
	2
Prompt Level _____	1
	5
	4
_____	3
	2
Prompt Level _____	1
	5
	4
_____	3
	2
Prompt Level _____	1
	5
	4
_____	3
	2
Prompt Level _____	1

Idea 4

Idea 5
Your Turn To Imitate

Idea 4, Learn To Imitate, Imitate To Learn, discusses the importance of teaching students with autism to imitate. Although teaching students to imitate adults is important, research also supports adults imitating children with autism. This is especially important for young children whose communication skills are just developing. Interventions that include imitating young children with autism have resulted in improvements in joint attention and shared positive affect as well as increases in eye gaze that regulates actions.

Here are some strategies for increasing your imitations.

❶ **Structure face-to-face activities.** Many teachers of preschoolers spend lots of time on the floor, at eye level with their students. This is a great way to encourage young students with autism to interact, and it also provides a format for imitating what the young student does. For example, if the child pushes the truck, the adult should push the truck. If the child rolls a ball, the adult should do the same. In addition, the adult should add language to the activity with simple words like, "Go, truck" or "Roll the ball." This talk labels both objects and activities for the child.

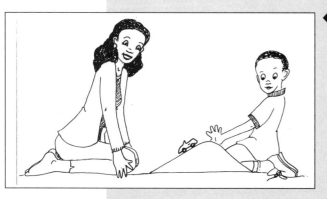

❷ **Use play.** During play, imitate sounds the child may make when excited. Also imitate actions and reactions. If possible engage the child in turn taking during the play to encourage their participation. Simple play like stacking blocks, pounding on a pan with a wooden spoon, or playing in sand can all elicit language and purposeful activities from young students.

❸ **Use touch.** Gently tickle the child to elicit sounds. As soon as you hear sounds, repeat them. When repeating, orient your face close enough to the student to have eye contact and to ensure that he or she is part of the dynamic. If the child likes to move, play chase (tag) or a simple version of Simon Says.

4 Use music. Music is always a great vehicle for stimulating activity and encouraging communication. Focus on songs that have predictable, repeated phrases, rhythms, and actions. When the student moves, you move; when he or she makes a sound, you repeat it. Eventually, you will want to pause and let the young student "fill in the blank" with spontaneous sounds and actions.

5 Use big movements and an enthusiastic communication style. If students enjoy gross motor activities, especially outdoors, add sounds and motions to the directions. For example, if a student wants to swing, begin to teach a simple directive like the sign for "more" or the word "go." If the student initiates either directive, imitate him and then push him on the swing immediately. Use exaggerated movements and an enthusiastic tone of voice to encourage the student to engage in turn taking with you. If the student makes a movement or sound, repeat it several times and show your excitement with smiles and verbal praise.

Idea 6
Your Turn, My Turn

Students with autism spectrum disorders often have deficits in the areas of social interaction and language use. Both of these domains can be addressed by structuring situations that encourage turn taking and reciprocal interactions.

Here's how to begin the process.

❶ Brainstorm a list of age appropriate activities that two people can do together and easily take turns. Examples include
- Building something with blocks
- Completing a puzzle
- Setting the table or stacking dishes
- Kicking a soccer ball back and forth
- Playing a simple card game like Uno or war
- Filling a glass and then emptying it
- Turning the pages of a book
- Coloring or painting a picture
- Dropping items into a bucket or plastic tub
- Singing a repeated phrase or clapping in rhythm

❷ Decide on a logical sequence of language to use while doing the activity. Think of words that make sense when used in the context of the activity and are also easy to repeat and remember. Use the phrases each time you do the activity, then pause and wait for the student to repeat after you. Provide special encouragement when students use pronouns correctly because this can be problematic for students with autism. Examples include
- My turn. Now your turn.
- Mine. Yours.
- First you (or the student's name: First Bobby). Then me (or your name: Then Mrs. Jones).
- Now you. Now me.
- Whose turn? That's right, Andrea's turn.

❸ Reinforce the student with enthusiastic praise every time he or she takes a turn and even more enthusiasm if the language that you have modeled is used. Coupons are provided to use as reinforcement.

 Tip:

Share this idea with parents to reinforce turn taking in both the school and home environments.

30

Idea 6

Idea 7
Follow the Music

Music can enrich lives and is a great resource to use with students with autism spectrum disorders. Because music is built on patterns and is often repetitious, it can be comforting to persons with autism spectrum disorders. This idea presents three simple ways to use music to promote social and communicative interactions.

Here's how this idea works.

❶ Use music to help students imitate language. The importance of imitation was discussed in Idea 4, Learn to Imitate, Imitate to Learn. Make stick puppets for students to hold up while singing, and encourage them to sing along. Many children will more readily imitate a word that is sung rather than spoken. We have provided two patterns for stick puppets. Use the spider when singing The Teensy Weensy Spider, and use the lamb when singing Mary Had a Little Lamb.

❷ Play music, especially songs with action words, to improve a student's receptive language. Many songs require participants to respond to simple commands. Sit across from the students and begin with simple melodies. Model and prompt the actions. As students progress, give them musical instruments and sing a song about actions that can be done with the instruments (e.g., this is the way we ring the bell).

❸ Use music to prompt students to specific actions. For example, use a simple melody to signal students to put away their work. Use a different melody to signal students to line up quietly to go to lunch. Music can also be used to help students learn to imitate movements. While students listen and watch, make simple movements and sway to the music. Now prompt your students to imitate you. Use objects, such as toys or clothing, to make it more interesting.

There are many songs that are appropriate to use with young children. Following is a partial list of songs we recommend:

- The Teensy Weensy Spider
- The Wheels on the Bus
- Head, Shoulders, Knees, and Toes
- Open-Shut
- I'm a Little Teapot
- If You're Happy and You Know It
- The Hokey Pokey
- Mary Had a Little Lamb
- Old McDonald Had a Farm
- The Bear Went Over the Mountain
- The Ants Go Marching
- Row, Row, Row Your Boat
- Five Little Ducks

33

Idea 8

Games, Games, and More Games

Games are a great way of teaching many different skills. Games help students with autism spectrum disorders in several skill areas, including building social relationships, sharing enjoyment, improving turn taking skills, improving motor skills, and using language in meaningful ways. These games, many of which are classics, allow students and teachers to move, laugh, and have fun together while they address these important skills.

Keep in mind that students with autism spectrum disorders fare better in noncompetitive, nonteam activities. Cooperative games are better for these students because they do not have winners or losers. However, if a team game is used, the teacher should consider assigning the teams and not allowing students to choose. We have included some games to play. They begin with simple two-person games and progress to noncompetitive, more complex games.

Here are some fun games to play.

❶ **Hot potato.** Students sit in a circle. Pass a Nerf ball (the hot potato) as quickly as possible. Keep a count of how many times the hot potato is passed without being dropped, and try to beat the best score.

❷ **Pat-a-cake.** Sit across from the student and hold up your hands. Indicate to the student to do the same. Gently pat the student's hands and say, "pat-a-cake." Once the student understands how to play, add music and other hand gestures such as claps and snaps.

❸ **Rock-paper-scissors.** Teach the student that a fist is rock, a flat hand is paper, and two pointing fingers are scissors. Rock always beats scissors; paper always beats rock; and scissors always beats paper. Sit or stand across from the student. Both players begin with a fist. With your fists, beat out a count of three, and then make a fist (rock), a flat hand (paper), or two pointing fingers (scissors). We recommend not keeping score. Instead play several times using enthusiastic verbal praise.

Note. This idea is adapted from *Practical Ideas That Really Work for Students with Asperger Syndrome,* by K. McConnell and G. R. Ryser, 2005, Austin, TX: PRO-ED. Copyright 2005 by PRO-ED, Inc. Adapted with permission.

④ Peek-a-boo. Sit across from the student and cover your eyes with your hands. Say, "Where is Jackie (or the student's name)?" Remove your hands and say, "There she is! Peek-a-boo!" Prompt the student to cover his or her eyes and imitate the process. You can also use a scarf or other cloth to cover your or the student's eyes. (Do not cover the student's eyes if he or she has tactile hypersensitivity.)

⑤ Gone fishing. Cut out fish shapes from heavy construction paper and attach a paper clip to each. Write a number or the students' names on each fish. Make simple string-and-stick fishing poles and attach a magnet to the end of each string. If using numbers, give each student a number and have everyone fish until each one catches their own fish.

⑥ Statue freeze. Students walk around the room or playground. When they hear a whistle or predetermined sound, they freeze like a statue until they hear the sound again.

⑦ Hawaiian hand clap. Students sit in a circle and set up a 1-2-3-4 rhythm by slapping their knees, clapping their hands, and snapping their fingers, first the right and then the left. Once the rhythm is established, the first player calls his or her name on the first snap and another name on the next snap. On the next sequence of snaps, the person whose name was called must call his or her own name and someone else's name. The object is to see how long the students can keep going without breaking the rhythm.

⑧ Who stole the cookies? This is another rhythm game similar to Hawaiian hand clap. Students sit in a circle and start a 1-2 rhythm, clapping once, then slapping their thighs once and repeating. When everyone is in sync, the teacher begins by saying in the rhythm, "Who stole the cookies from the cookie jar? (Name of student) stole the cookies from the cookie jar." The student named replies without losing the rhythm, "Who me?" All students reply, "Yes you." The student says, "Couldn't be." All students reply, "Then who?" The named person then takes up the chant by naming someone else.

⑨ Toss a name. Students stand in a circle. The first student has a Nerf ball and says, for example, "I am Nick and this is Shannon." The first student (Nick) throws the ball to the second student (Shannon), who repeats the process. The key is to not repeat anyone's name until all students' names have been called.

🎲 Tip:

As you play, talk the students through the game, require turn taking, and demonstrate your own enthusiasm.

Idea 9
Look in the Mirror

This idea is similar to video modeling, but the only equipment needed is a mirror. It is an effective and simple way to teach students with autism spectrum disorders to practice appropriate facial expressions and body language. In a safe and relaxed atmosphere, work with the student one-on-one in front of a mirror so he or she can get a sense of how he or she appears to others. Use mirror work to practice specific skills, such as

- making eye contact,
- using a variety of facial expressions for different purposes,
- standing in a relaxed fashion while talking to a friend,
- looking excited as someone shares their interest in something, and
- keeping hands still while talking or listening.

Here are some strategies to try while using the mirror.

❶ Demonstrate an expression, gesture, or movement, and ask the student to imitate it. Sit side-by-side, close enough for you both to completely see each other's face in the mirror.

❷ Name an emotion and ask the student to show you what it looks like.

❸ Model a feeling or intention with your body language or facial expression. Ask the student to identify how you are feeling.

❹ Let the student demonstrate a specific emotion by using body language, facial expressions, and gestures. Then, you guess what emotion he or she is demonstrating.

 Tip:

Use the tickets on the following page for positive reinforcement. Copy the tickets on sturdy paper. Decide how many times the student needs to exhibit the skill, then select the appropriate ticket and fill in the student's name and the target skill. Each time you see the student demonstrating the skill, punch one of the numbers. When all the numbers are punched, the student can turn in the ticket for a reward.

Name _____

Skill _____

1 **2** **3**

Name _____

Skill _____

1 **2** **3**

Name _____

Skill _____

1 **2** **3**

Name _____

Skill _____

1 **2** **3**

Name _____

Skill _____

1 **2** **3** **4**

Name _____

Skill _____

1 **2** **3** **4**

Name _____

Skill _____

1 **2** **3** **4**

Name _____

Skill _____

1 **2** **3** **4**

Name _____

Skill _____

1 **2** **3** **4** **5**

Name _____

Skill _____

1 **2** **3** **4** **5**

Name _____

Skill _____

1 **2** **3** **4** **5**

Name _____

Skill _____

1 **2** **3** **4** **5**

Idea 9

Idea 10
Schedule Sensory Time

Students with autism spectrum disorders often have sensitivity to sensory input, which can make it difficult to function in any environment. For example, a child with tactile sensitivity will experience difficulty with physical contact or touch. To increase a student's tolerance for physical contact, schedule time for you and the student to engage in an enjoyable activity that is tactile.

Here are some fun activities to try.

Use Water

Encourage the student to play in the water at a sink or water table. While he or she is playing, stand across from the student, lightly rippling the water and splashing gently. While the student's and your hands are both in the water, touch the student's hands lightly for brief periods of time. As time goes on, begin extending the touch time by playing with boats and other floating objects with the student.

Play in Sand or with Clay or Shaving Cream

Provide modeling or synthetic clay, sand, or shaving cream for students, until you find a texture that the student prefers. (Caution: If the student is likely to put any of these in his or her mouth, find another medium). While the student plays, put your hands in the sand, clay, or cream, wiggling your fingers, gently sifting the sand, or helping the student mold an object. While assisting the student, gently touch his or her hands for brief periods of time, extending this time as the student grows more comfortable.

Use Everyday Gestures

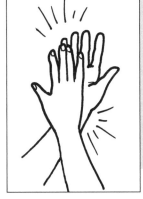

An easy way to help students get comfortable with touch is to use everyday touches that communicate. Gestures like "high fives," handshakes, hugs, and pats on the back communicate approval, enjoyment, and encouragement, so they not only increase tolerance for touch but can be reinforcing as well. Encourage parents to use them at home as well.

For Older Students

If you want to continue to encourage students to tolerate touch when they are older, consider these additional ideas:

- Take turns playing electronic or video games with button or stick controllers. Guide the student's hands by lightly placing your hand over his or her hand.

- Use musical instruments to encourage touching. For example, playing the piano together can help students if you gradually increase your physical guidance.

- The computer mouse is a great tool. Students often need assistance and will tolerate physical touch because they enjoy the computer games or programs so much.

- Don't forget shared reading. Whether you are looking at a magazine or reading a book, you can take turns turning pages and pointing to pictures, as well as sitting close to each other.

Idea 11
Bring Out the Noise

When children learn to talk, they begin by making sounds like laughter, cries, or single sounds that do not really have meaning. These vocalizations serve an important purpose, because they provide a basis for reciprocal interaction. Parents and caregivers often mimic and repeat the child's sounds while smiling, tickling, and touching the child.

When students with autism are nonverbal, it can be difficult for teachers to stimulate them to make noises, small sounds, or laughter. However, encouraging vocalizations is important so that students begin the language development process.

Here are some ways to bring out the noise.

❶ Tickling the student

❷ Blowing bubbles, especially near the student's face

❸ Playing music or musical instruments

❹ Playing hide and seek or peek-a-boo

❺ Repeating rhymes and chants, along with gestures and movements

❻ Talking through puppets

❼ Hugging, swinging, or gently lifting the student into the air

🦗 Tip:

As soon as you hear the student make some sounds, repeat them back to the student, then clap praise, cheer, smile, and make a big fuss to encourage the student to say more.

Idea 12
When/Do Books

Many students with autism are rigid in their patterns of behavior. It can be very difficult to teach them to modify their behaviors to fit various situations. However, because expectations and rules in school change often, depending on the teacher, type of activity, size of the class, location, or other variables, students with autism must learn to adapt. To help students meet behavioral expectations in a variety of environments, you can use a two- or three-part book with visual examples and explanations. These teacher-made When/Do books are great tools for representing and teaching the rules for more than one situation in school. The idea is to show and explain to students that "*When* they are _____ they should *do* _____."

Here is how to make and use the books.

❶ Fold a piece of paper in half and then in half again.

❷ Unfold the book and cut up the inside center line toward the top. If you want three sections instead of two, make two cuts.

❸ Write the word "When" on the top of each flap, and place a picture, symbol or word that represents a setting that the student will encounter. The second flap should represent the a situation that might occur in that setting. In our example for Aaron, we put "PE" on the front of the first flap and "Drink from Fountain" on the front of the second flap.

 Tip:

To make your When/Do book sturdier, you can laminate it and then recut the flap line.

◆ Under each flap, put one or more pictures, symbols, or words that represent the behavioral rules for that situation. For example, in PE, Aaron must line up quietly when getting a drink from the fountain, so we placed a picture and the rule representing this. Before he goes to PE, his teacher will remind him that the rule in PE when getting a drink at the fountain is to line up quietly.

Idea 13
Puppet Play

Students with autism or related disorders often fail to play with others and usually do not spontaneously engage in make-believe play. One way to encourage play is to use puppets. There are many shapes, sizes, and types of puppets, from simple finger puppets to elaborate marionettes. We have provided several easy ways to create puppets for play. They are fun to use and are great tools for encouraging make-believe play, language development, and socialization.

Here are some ways to use puppets with students.

Make-Believe Play

❶ *Act out favorite events.* Choose a favorite event of the child's and act it out using the puppets. For example, you might pretend you are at a birthday party blowing out candles and singing happy birthday.

❷ *Make up stories.* Make up a story or act one out from a script using the puppets as the characters. Begin with a short scene and add to it as your student(s) become comfortable.

❸ *Put motions to songs or rhymes.* Using the puppets, put motions to familiar songs or rhymes. This is a great way to engage children who are nonverbal.

Language Development

❶ *Hold a conversation.* At first, you may have to do the talking for both puppets, yours and the student's. Talk about school, home, favorite toys, favorite people, and so on.

❷ *Practice familiar songs or rhymes.* Repeat songs, nursery rhymes, poems, or jingles. Have the puppets take turns or use this as a choral activity in which all puppets perform the same action while singing or saying the same thing.

❸ *Ask questions.* Have your puppet ask the student's puppet some easy questions that require short answers. At first, ask questions you are sure the student can answer. As the student becomes comfortable, ask increasingly more complex questions.

Socialization

❶ *Reinforce social skills.* After teaching a social skill to the class or a small group of students, use the puppets to reinforce the skill. Choose one social skill, such as initiating a conversation and model the skill using your puppet. Prompt the child to respond. Next, have the child model the skill using his or her puppet.

❷ *Imitate actions.* Model an action (e.g., waving goodbye). Prompt the child to imitate you. Once the child is comfortable with the process, switch roles.

❸ *Role-play social or unfamiliar situations.* Use the puppets to role play how to act in different social situations (e.g., going to a friend's birthday party). You can also role play situations that are unfamiliar to the child (e.g., attending a session with a new therapist).

Resources

Aunt Annie's Crafts, Puppets Around the World. Purchase a Windows program for making several types of puppets. Instructions are provided for making a few of the puppets at this Web site.
www.auntannie.com/puppets/index.html

Pakaluk Puppets. Creators of lightweight hand puppets that are easy to manipulate, especially for children.
www.pakalukpuppets.com

Playful Puppets. Unique puppets that can actually swallow objects.
www.playfulpuppets.com

Puppet Artists. Individually designed and made puppets, from finger puppets to marionettes.
www.puppetartists.com

Puppetools: Advancing the Language of Play. Offers workshops that show how to use puppets to promote play and language.
www.puppetools.com

Teaching with Puppets. Offers educational shows that combine music and puppetry.
www.1worldmusicandpuppets.com/teachingwith puppets.html

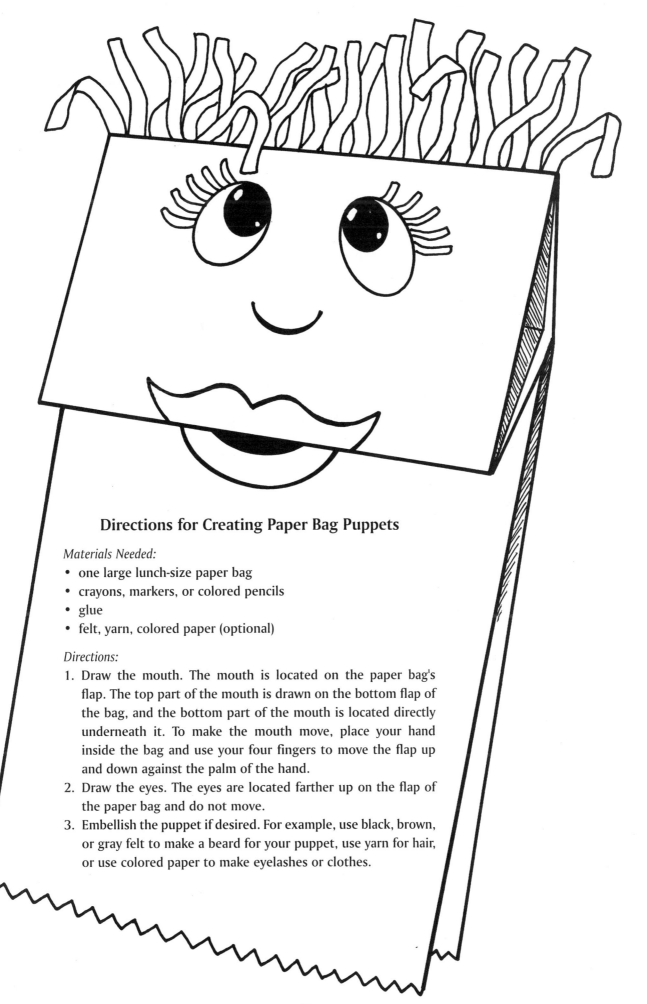

Directions for Creating Paper Bag Puppets

Materials Needed:
- one large lunch-size paper bag
- crayons, markers, or colored pencils
- glue
- felt, yarn, colored paper (optional)

Directions:

1. Draw the mouth. The mouth is located on the paper bag's flap. The top part of the mouth is drawn on the bottom flap of the bag, and the bottom part of the mouth is located directly underneath it. To make the mouth move, place your hand inside the bag and use your four fingers to move the flap up and down against the palm of the hand.

2. Draw the eyes. The eyes are located farther up on the flap of the paper bag and do not move.

3. Embellish the puppet if desired. For example, use black, brown, or gray felt to make a beard for your puppet, use yarn for hair, or use colored paper to make eyelashes or clothes.

Directions for Creating Sock Puppets

Sock puppets are easy and inexpensive to make. Save your old socks or use socks with no mates.

Materials Needed
- Sock
- Glue gun
- Scissors
- Paper
- Felt or construction paper
- Cardboard (e.g., from a cereal box)
- Mouth pattern
- Additional materials such as goggly eyes, cotton balls, yarn, and so on

Directions
1. Copy the mouth pattern onto the cardboard and cut it out. Fold the mouth in half.
2. Glue the felt or the construction paper to the mouth piece.
3. Place the sock on your hand so that your fingers and thumb are in the toe.
4. Cut a piece of the sock out between your thumb and fingers. This is for the mouth piece.
5. Attach (we suggest you use the glue gun) the mouth piece to the sock where the opening is.

Make the puppet anything you want. Think about adding eyes, hair, mustaches, neckties, shirts, beards, hats, and so on.

Mouth Pattern

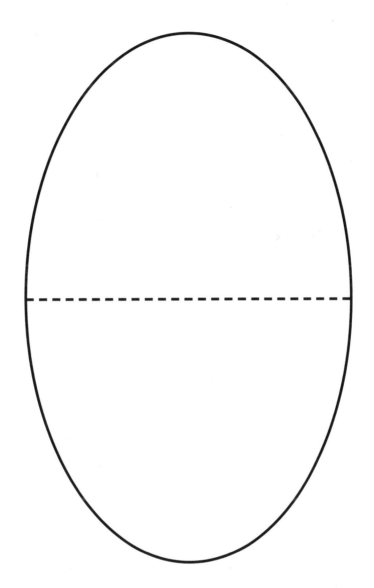

Idea 13

Directions for Creating Paper Finger Puppets

Use two of your fingers to represent the legs of these simple paper puppets. You can make paper finger puppets by following the directions below and using the patterns found on the next page, or you can draw your own.

Materials Needed
- Stiff paper
- Scissors
- Markers, colored pencils, or crayons
- Glue
- Additional materials such as goggly eyes, cotton balls, yarn, and so on.

Directions
1. Copy one of the puppet patterns, or draw your own puppet on the stiff paper.
2. Color the pattern using the markers, pencils, or crayons.
3. Cut out the puppet, including the finger holes.
4. Decorate the puppet by adding eyes, yarn for hair, or other materials.

Idea 13

Directions for Creating Stick Puppets

You can make simple stick puppets by following the directions below or use the patterns found on the next page. If you use the patterns, simply color, cut out, and glue them on a popsicle stick, dowel, plastic straw, or other suitable stick.

Styrofoam Ball Stick Puppets

Materials Needed
- Two styrofoam balls, a small one for the head and a larger one for the body
- Eyes
- Colored pipe cleaners
- Glue
- Dowel
- Felt, markers, yarn (optional)

Directions
1. Connect the two styrofoam balls together with three or four short pipe cleaners.
2. Use pipe cleaners to make arms and legs.
3. Glue eyes on small styrofoam ball.
4. Embellish by adding features such as mouth, hair or clothing using felt, markers, or yarn. This lets your audience know what the puppet is supposed to represent. You can make a wide variety of puppets this way, including humans and animals.
5. Connect the bottom of the body to the dowel.

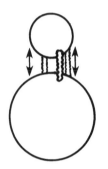

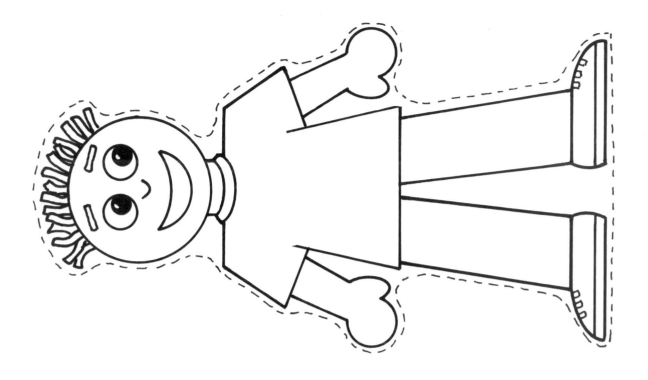

Idea 14
Get Predictable

We know that learning to use language in reading, writing, and talking is an interactive process. One strategy for encouraging students to improve their language skills is to use predictable or patterned books. Predictable books are usually colorful, engaging, and fun to read, so they are a great motivator for students with any level of language proficiency. These patterned books provide students with autism an extra bonus: an opportunity for social interaction while taking turns reading with their teacher.

Here's how to use the books.

❶ Sit close.

❷ Read aloud.

❸ Frequently wait for the student to "fill in the blank" by saying the missing word or phrase.

Make things more challenging.

❶ Ask students to identify people and things in the pictures.

❷ Point to pictures to identify objects.

❸ Repeat aloud what you have read.

Because many students with autism are good at repeating what they hear, this process is a natural fit for their learning style. We have provided a list of 20 of our favorite patterned or predictable books to help you get started.

Patterned or Predictable Books

Alexander and the Terrible, Horrible, No Good, Very Bad Day by Judith Viorst

Are you my Mother? by P. D. Eastman

Benny's Pennies by Pat Brisson

Brown Bear, Brown Bear by Bill Martin

Drummer Hoff by Barbara Emberly

Frog Went A-Courtin' by John Langstaff

Hush Little Baby illustrated by Aliki

In Enzo's Splendid Gardens by Patricia Polacco

Just for You by Mercer Mayer

Papa's Going to Buy Me a Mockingbird by Don Higgins

The Fat Cat by Jack Kent

The Gingerbread Man by Jan Richards

The Little Red Hen by Paul Galdone

The Napping House by Audrey Wood

The Runaway Bunny by Margaret Wise Brown

The Very Busy Spider by Eric Carle

The Very Hungry Caterpillar by Eric Carle

Today is Monday by Eric Carle

Where the Wild Things Are by Maurice Sendak

Whose Mouse Are You? By Robert Kraus

For an extensive list of patterned books, see

Teaching Reading Creatively: Reading and Writing as Communication, 7th ed. (Appendix N), by Frank B. May, 2006, Upper Saddle River, NJ: Prentice Hall.

Predictable Books. http://www.earlyliterature.ecsd.net/predictable_books.htm

Idea 15
Yes or No

Indicating a yes or no response is an important skill for students. Whether they do so by nodding or shaking their head, pointing, saying or signing the words *yes* or *no*, or using some other signal such as pushing a red or green light, the important lesson for students is that their meaningful use of some form of language produces a result. This idea uses cards to prompt the student to indicate his or her preferences.

Here's how it works.

❶ Copy the Yes cards on green paper and the No cards on red paper.

❷ Identify three or four items that you are certain the student will want and three or four items that the student will not want.

❸ Present an item that the student will want and say, "Do you want this?" Point to the Yes cue card and, if needed, prompt the student to indicate yes, and give the item to the student. If the student does not indicate yes, model it, then wait for the student's response.

❹ After the student has completed several successful trials indicating yes, present an item that the student will not want. Repeat the procedures above using the "no" cue card. (When the student indicates no, remove the item.)

❺ Gradually phase out your modeling and just use the appropriate cue card as a visual prompt. Work toward phasing out the cue cards as well.

☜ Tip:

If a student is nonverbal, teach the student to point to or hold up the card indicating his or her preference. Once mastery is attained, provide a laminated set of the yes and no cards for him or her to use.

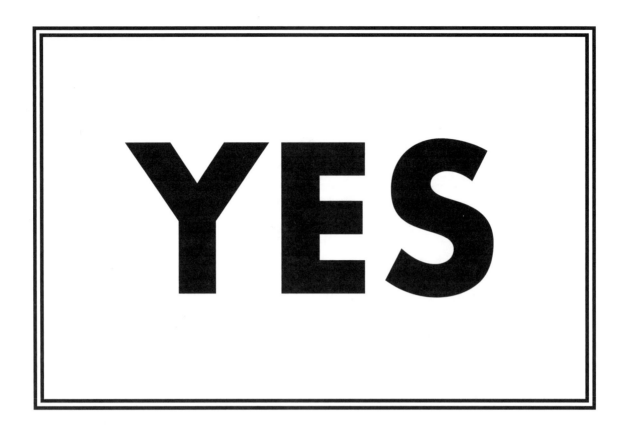

Idea 15

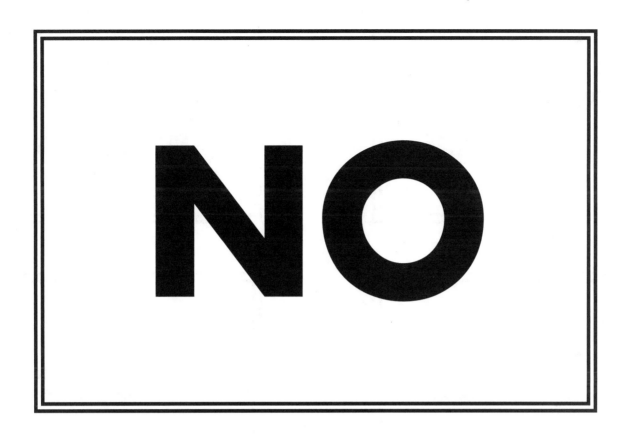

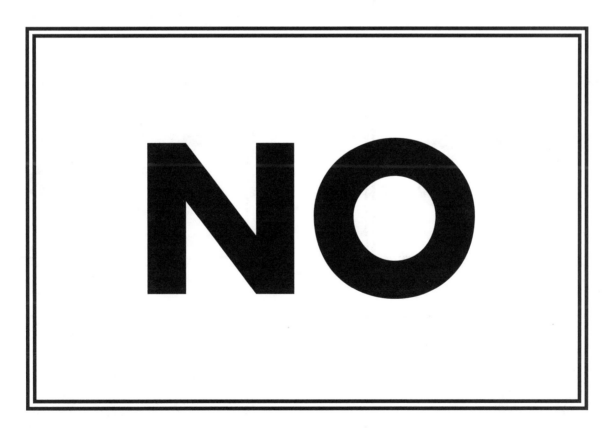

YES

YES

YES

YES

YES

YES

YES

YES

Idea 15

Idea 16
Cueing Pronouns

Children typically begin to use pronouns such as *I, you,* and *my* when they are about 18 to 24 months old. Children with autism spectrum disorders often do not but engage instead in the speech pattern of echolalia. In echolalia speech, the student repeats what he or she has heard rather than responding meaningfully with a pronoun. For example,

Ms. Jones: "Whose toy is this?"

Billy: "Whose toy is this?" Instead of, "My toy."

Students with autistic spectrum disorders may engage in echolalia because of their limitations in joint attention. Joint attention is the shared attention between two people on an object or event and is considered to be a prerequisite for language development.

Teaching pronouns can be difficult because the pronoun one uses is dependent on who is speaking to whom. Suppose you are trying to teach a student to use the pronoun *my.* You must remember to reinforce the student with, "That's right! My toy." and not by saying, "That's right! It's your toy." In this idea, we use pronoun cue cards to teach students to use the correct pronoun when responding to questions. Teach the pronouns *I* and *me* first, then *my, mine,* and *your.* Once the student demonstrates mastery of these five pronouns, phase in other pronouns (e.g., *her, his, their, us*).

Here's how it works.

❶ Ask the student a question, and point to the pronoun cue card you want the student to use. For example, "What is this?" while holding up a toy that belongs to the child. Point to the "My" cue card, and if needed, prompt the child to say "my."

❷ If the student does not complete the rest of the response (e.g., "My toy") model it, then wait for the student's response.

❸ Gradually phase out your verbal modeling and just use the appropriate cue card as a visual prompt. Work toward phasing out the cue cards as well.

🍥 Tip:

Teach students to use additional communication behaviors, such as pointing and looking at the person or object, to further clarify the referent.

63

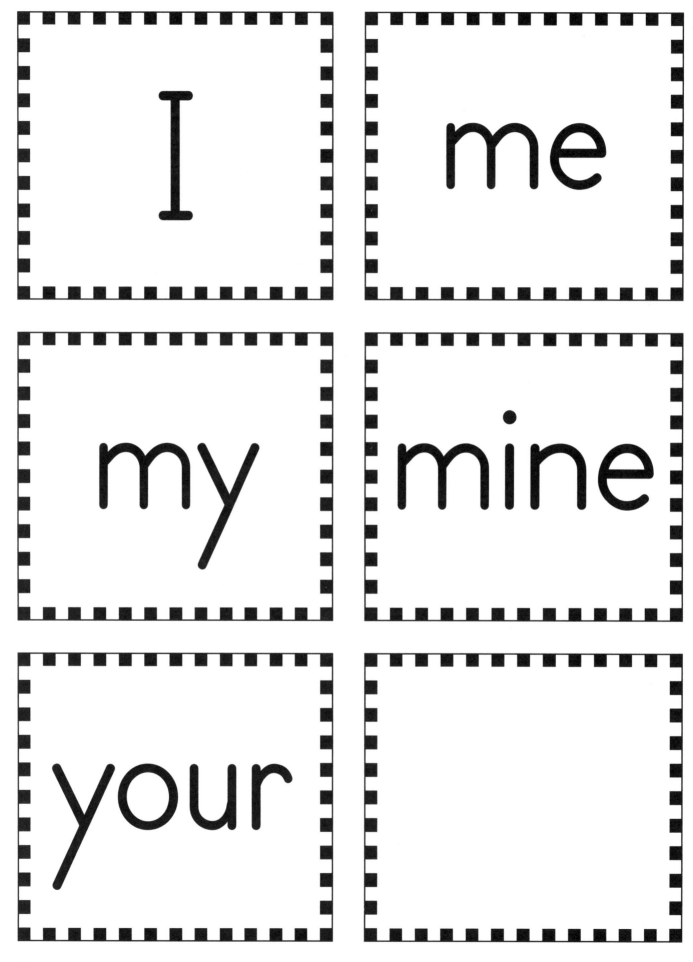

I

me

my

mine

your

64

Idea 17

Touch, Show, Find, or Say

Teachers always strive to improve students' receptive and expressive language skills. Receptive language is important because when students understand what teachers or family members say they can follow verbal directions, comprehend instruction, identify objects, and demonstrate their understanding of everyday conversations. Expressive language is important for independence. When students can communicate with others, they can express their needs and wants, ask questions, and convey meaning. Good receptive and expressive language allow students to participate more actively in the world around them.

Receptive Language

One strategy for increasing receptive language is to teach students to demonstrate that they know the meanings of commonly used words by touching, showing, or finding objects. After the student has mastered a basic set of vocabulary words and can identify them correctly every time, begin to use two objects at a time. This will require the student to discriminate between the two. If he or she still chooses the correct object, you will be more sure that the student really knows the meaning of the word. To encourage even more generalization and to expand your teaching away from the table or desk, begin to give the student a direction to "Find _____" in the classroom, all over the school, in the community, and at home. This will require the student to discriminate among several different objects and increase the possibilities for a large and ever-expanding vocabulary.

Expressive Language

One strategy for increasing expressive language is to teach students to say the name of the object, person, place, or activity. Once the student can say the names of items correctly, you can encourage higher level language development by asking him or her to identify things based on the following:

- *Function* (Tell me what you eat with. That's right, a spoon.)
- *Category* (Tell me the people in your family. Good. Mama, Daddy.)
- *Form* (Tell me something that is round. A ball. That's right.)

Here are the two components of Touch, Show, Find, or Say.

Decide on the Words to Teach.

❶ Decide on the categories of words you want the student to learn. These could include family members, people at school, commonly used toys or materials, items of clothing, and so on.

❷ For as many words as possible, locate the actual objects (e.g., the student's favorite toy, an article of clothing).

❸ Take photographs or find pictures to represent the words that are too large or unavailable (e.g., pictures of family members, advertisements with names of restaurants).

❹ Arrange the photos, pictures, or objects by categories. Start with the most familiar categories.

Use a Systematic Teaching Model.

❶ Have your first set of photos, pictures, or objects ready to use. At a table or desk, sit across from or next to the student.

❷ Select the first word you would like to teach (e.g., *Mom*, represented by a photograph of the student's mother).

❸ Show the object, picture, or photograph to the student. As you do so, touch it and say the word slowly and clearly (e.g., "Mom").

❹ Ask the student to "touch" or "show you" or "say" the item (e.g., "Show me Mom." "Say Mom."). If necessary, guide his or her hand gently or prompt with beginning sounds (e.g., "mmm").

❺ As soon as the student touches or says the item, reinforce him or her immediately with praise, smiles, cheers, and, if necessary, a tangible reinforcer.

❻ Repeat the procedure five to ten times, depending on the age and instructional level of the student.

❼ Ask the student to touch or say the item, but this time do not prompt or guide his or her hand (e.g., "Touch Mom" or "Say Mom").

❽ If the student responds by touching the object or photograph or saying the word, reinforce him or her immediately. If the student does not respond correctly, repeat the teaching sequence.

🌺 Tip:

Some students with autism spectrum disorders are completely nonverbal or have very limited oral language skills. For those students, you may wish to begin expressive language by encouraging production of sounds (See Idea 11, Bring Out the Noise). However, if the student is already saying some words and you believe he or she has the prerequisite skills to use language in more meaningful and consistent ways, then try this idea. Introduce one word at a time, beginning with those you have already heard him or her say.

We have provided several materials to help you teach the important skills of receptive and expressive language:

- A list of commonly used vocabulary words, grouped into categories. This list should help you get started by giving you ideas of what words to teach. Of course, you should start small and keep expanding.

- A list of resources for drawings and photographs that can be used to teach receptive and expressive language.

- A data collection form to use when teaching words. Here's how it works.
  1. Choose a target word or words.
  2. Find cards or everyday objects that depict the target words.
  3. Circle *receptive* or *expressive*, depending on which type of skill you are teaching.
  4. Circle the appropriate skill level.
     I = **Introduce** (*At this level, the child does not consistently demonstrate understanding of the word.*)
     M = **Mastery** (*At this level, the child demonstrates understanding of the word at a predetermined mastery level. We suggest you use 85%.*)
     T = **Transfer** (*At this level, the child demonstrates understanding of the word across situations.*)

- Sample vocabulary cards in Appendix A. These are drawings of common vocabulary words you may want to teach students. You should use the real object whenever possible, but using photographs or drawings is sometimes necessary.

Categories and Words

People at Home (teach by name)
Mother/Mom
Father/Dad
Stepparents
Brother(s)
Sister(s)
Grandparents
Extended family members
Family friends
Family pets

People at School (teach by name)
Teachers
Assistants or Aides
Principal or Director
Classmates
Bus driver
Cafeteria personnel
Speech therapist
Occupational or Physical therapist
Volunteers/Helpers

Items of Clothing
Pants/Slacks
Shorts
Top or Shirt
Blouse
Belt
Socks
Shoes
Pajamas/Bathrobe
Underpants/Shorts
Bra or T-shirt
Bathing suit

Food
The student's favorite foods (teach these first)
Milk
Soft drinks/Sodas (by name)
Sandwich
Taco
Hamburger
Pizza
Spaghetti
French fries
Cereal
Bread
Tortilla
Cheese

Chips
Pretzels
Apple
Banana
Pear
Orange
(any others common to the student's home or school)

Toys, Games, Hobbies
Ball
Swing
Bicycle
Puzzle
Car
Truck
Keys
Doll
Drum
Game
TV
VCR
Video
CD or tape

Places
Home
Grandparents' or other relatives' house
Grocery store
Bank
Favorite restaurants (with logo)
Park
Doctor's office
School
Church
Playground

Emergency/Safety Words
Stop
Go
Walk
Boys'/Men's Room
Girls'/Women's Room
Poison
Danger/Dangerous
Caution
In
Out

Other Categories of Words
- Most common words in reading. These lists are especially good for students who have prereading skills. They include the Dolch words and the Allen List.
- Colors
- Numbers (not counting objects, just recognizing the number)
- Animals
- Household objects
- Items of furniture
- Rooms in the home or school
- Adjectives (especially feelings)
- Verbs (especially action verbs)

Resources for Picture and Word Cards

The following products are available from PRO-ED, Inc.

Comprehensive Receptive and Expressive Vocabulary Test—Second Edition (CREVT–2)
Photo Picture Book
- The picture book is sprial-bound and has 10 full-color picture plates, six pictures per plate. Each plate relates to a theme: animals, transportation, occupations, clothing, food, personal grooming, tools, household appliances, recreation, and clerical materials.

Test of Language Development—Intermediate (TOLD–I:3)
Picture Book
- The picture book is sprial-bound and has 9 full-color picture plates, six pictures per plate.

Silly Sentences
- The complete program includes three individually color-coded decks of cards and an instruction booklet in a vinyl storage envelope.

Basic Vocabulary Study Cards
- This program is designed to teach students the sight recognition of 600 basic vocabulary words (nouns and verbs) through the manipulation of picture and word cards. The complete program includes a direction manual, vocabulary list, the card sets, record sheet, and pre- posttest card.

Library of Vocabulary Photographs—Second Edition
- The complete program includes 13 picture groups; each group consists of 47 full-color photos of everyday and not-so-everyday items. Each picture group is in a vinyl envelope.

500 Thematic Lists and Activities for Language Expansion
- This comprehensive manual offers a large supply of reproducible thematic pictures and skill-building activities.

Target Word Competency Chart

Name _____

I = Introduce
M = Master
T = Transfer

Circle the level of competence for *receptive expressive* use of the target word.

Date	Target Word	Competence Level	Evaluation
		I M T	
		I M T	
		I M T	
		I M T	
		I M T	
		I M T	
		I M T	
		I M T	
		I M T	
		I M T	
		I M T	
		I M T	
		I M T	
		I M T	
		I M T	
		I M T	
		I M T	
		I M T	
		I M T	
		I M T	
		I M T	
		I M T	
		I M T	

Idea 17

Idea 18
Wh– Game

Encouraging students with autism spectrum disorders to engage in meaningful back-and-forth conversation can be difficult. This lack of conversation affects both social relationships and opportunities to learn and practice language skills. One way to help students get started with conversations is to play the Wh– game.

Here's how it works.

❶ Use the cube template provided to make the die.

❷ Choose a topic that interests the student, and have the student roll the die.

❸ Whatever word the die lands on, the student must ask a question about the topic using that word. If the die lands on the question mark, the student may choose any wh– word with which to begin his or her question.

❹ The teacher or peer who is playing with the student answers the question and asks the student another question using the same wh– word. Once the student responds, the student can roll the die again.

🌺 Tip:

Show the student a photo of a place or person that he or she frequents or sees on a regular basis. Have the student ask the wh– questions about that place or person.

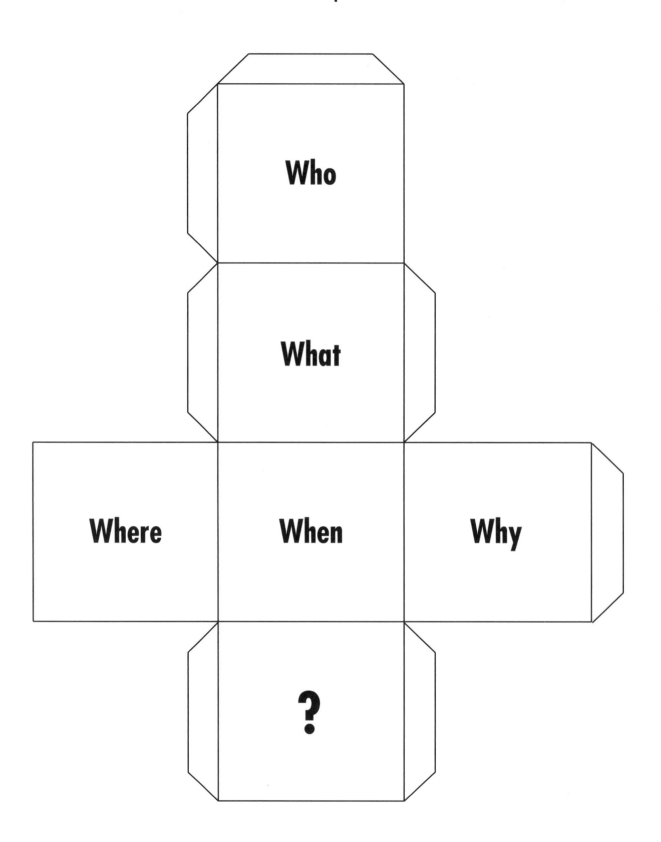

Who

What

Where   When   Why

?

Idea 18

Idea 19
Talk Prompters

Three functions of communicating emerge in normally developing children in the first year of their life: behavior regulation, social interactions, and joint attention. Children with autism spectrum disorders have difficulty using communication for social interactions and joint attention. This in turn, limits their language development and ability to form peer relationships. Therefore, these functions must be taught systematically.

Talk prompters can be used to help students learn to use language for social interaction, particularly, initiating and maintaining conversation. Use the Talk Prompters to teach verbal students how to begin and extend a conversation. The Talk Prompters on the following pages are designed to be used as conversation openers and extenders, and can be used to teach these important communication skills.

Each card is designed to be two sided. (Copy the Opener Cards on one side, and copy the Extender Cards on the other side.) Side 1 is called the Opener and has an O at the top of the card. Side 2 is called the Extender and has an E at the top of the card. Each side has a prompt (word phrase) followed by a blank. Below the blank are several words or word phrases that can be placed into the blank.

O

What did you _____?
- eat for lunch
- do today
- learn in school this week
- do for fun last night

What did you like about what you _____? E
- ate for lunch
- did today
- learned in school this week
- did for fun last night

Here's how to use Talk Prompters.

❶ Take any card and turn it to the Opener side. For example: The "What's your favorite _____?" prompt is followed by four suggestions: dessert, TV show, game, time of day. Model for the students how to take each word or word phrase and complete the question.

❷ Turn the card over to the Extender side. Model for the students how to extend the conversation by repeating the phrase.

❸ Have the students break into pairs to practice using the prompts. Try using one prompt per week.

⚜ Tip:

Copy, laminate, and place the cards on a small ring. Give each child a set. Break the children into pairs and let them practice.

What's your favorite _____?

- TV show
- dessert
- game
- animal

What do you do when you are _____?

- scared
- happy
- excited
- sad

What did you _____?

- eat for lunch
- do today
- learn in school this week
- do for fun last night

What is the name of _____?

- your best friend
- the city you live in
- your teacher at school
- the school you go to

Where did you go _____?

- for the weekend
- last night
- for your birthday
- after school

Where could I go to _____?

- find a good book
- buy groceries
- play a game
- get an ice-cream cone

Idea 19

Extender Cards

How do you feel when you are _____ ?

- scared
- happy
- excited
- sad

E

What do you like best about your favorite _____ ?

- TV show
- dessert
- game
- animal

E

What is one thing you like about _____ ?

- your best friend
- the city you live in
- your teacher at school
- the school you go to

E

What did you like about what you _____ ?

- ate for lunch
- did today
- learned in school this week
- did for fun last night

E

How do I get to the place where I could _____ ?

- find a good book
- buy groceries
- play a game
- get an ice-cream cone

E

What did you do _____ ?

- for the weekend
- last night
- for your birthday
- after school

E

75

Idea 19

Idea 20

Conversation Cards

Many students with autism or related disorders need to improve their language and social skills in everyday social situations. Whether greeting someone, asking introductory questions, sharing information, or just making polite conversation, it helps if students know about people in their lives, including the person's name and something about him or her (e.g., occupation, hobby, family information).

To help prepare a student for conversation, create a card file. Each card can provide a name, photo, and basic information about a friend, classmate, coworker, family member, neighbor, teacher, bus driver, therapist, or acquaintance. Use the cards to teach and prepare students *before* they encounter people in social situations. Students can practice saying names, greeting, asking and answering relevant questions, and saying goodbye.

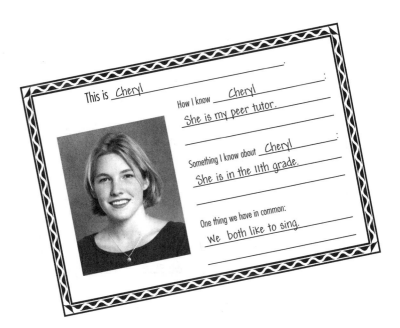

This is _____.

How I know _____:

_____

_____

Something I know about _____:

_____

_____

One thing we have in common:

_____

_____

(photo)

This is _____.

How I know _____:

_____

_____

Something I know about _____:

_____

_____

One thing we have in common:

_____

_____

(photo)

Idea 20

Idea 21
Problem Solve with I Think, You Think

Many students with autism find it difficult to solve problems, especially when the problems require an understanding of someone else's feelings, point of view, or attitude. As part of social skills instruction, teachers or therapists often teach students how to recognize others' feelings or attitudes, compare them to their own, and then figure out how to reconcile their differences. We have provided a simple graphic that can be used to represent a problem, how each student feels or what they think, and then a solution. You can use the Problem Solve with I Think, You Think form as the basis for teaching, discussion, and practice when focusing on problem solving.

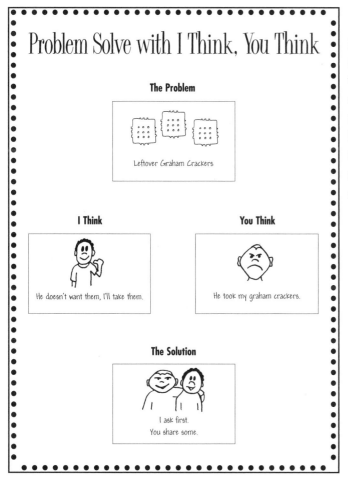

Example

Nick finishes his snack of graham crackers and wants some of Ramon's, which are still left because Ramon does not like graham crackers. Nick takes Ramon's crackers, and Ramon has a fit. Nick is therefore taught to ask first, and Ramon is taught to share some, but not all, of his leftover graham crackers.

Problem Solve with I Think, You Think

The Problem

I Think

You Think

The Solution

Idea 21

Idea 22
The Daily Scoop

All parents and teachers want to be able to communicate with their children or students. Sharing information, whether about school or home, builds relationships and provides a basis for improving language skills. In addition, a good home-school communication system helps ensure that everyone knows what is happening in a student's life and should prevent misunderstandings.

The Daily Scoop provides an easy to use, convenient format for home-school communication. You can use any one of several formats to help students share what they have done, where they have gone, whom they have seen, and so on. Teachers and parents can send these sheets back and forth daily. We hope that the convenient format will ensure their consistent use.

The Daily Scoop

Directions: Use pictures, symbols, or words to communicate the events that occurred at home.

Date _____

At home I:

_____

_____

_____

Idea 22

The Daily Scoop

Directions: Use pictures, symbols, or words to communicate the events that occurred at home.

Date _____

At school I:

_____

_____

_____

Idea 22

The Daily Scoop

Directions: Create a menu of pictures, symbols, or words that can be circled by the student each day.

Date _____

Today I ate:

orange

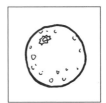
raisins

cookie

pizza

sandwich

chips

Today I went to these classes:

Reading

Music

PE

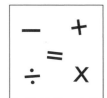
Math

Today I saw these people:

the bus driver

my teacher

my friend

Idea 22

The Daily Scoop

Directions: Create a menu of pictures, symbols, or words that can be circled by the student each day.

Date _____

Today I ate:

☐	☐	☐	☐
___	___	___	___
☐	☐	☐	☐
___	___	___	___

Today I went to these classes:

☐	☐	☐	☐	☐
___	___	___	___	___

Today I saw these people:

☐	☐	☐	☐	☐
___	___	___	___	___

Idea 22

The Daily Scoop

Directions: Create a menu of pictures, symbols, or words that can be circled by the student each day.

Date _____

Today I ate:

Today I went to these classes:

Today I saw these people:

Idea 22

Idea 23
Choice Cards

Students with autism spectrum disorders often fail to indicate their preference or interest in daily activities or everyday objects. This lack of enthusiasm and communication may isolate students from their peers and family members. One simple way to help students begin the process of sharing their interests is to teach them to indicate their choice of two or more options. By making choices, students begin to express preferences and learn the importance of communciation: They will get what they want more often if they make a choice.

Choice Cards are a simple tool to help you teach students to express a preference or make a choice. The teacher structures the choices, and then students are required to select what they want. Use the cards on the following pages throughout the day to encourage students to tell you what they want to do, where they would like to go, what they want to eat or drink, when they want to go somewhere, and so forth. After students make a choice between two options, begin to expand to three or four options. Fill in the blanks with photographs, symbols (like those from the Mayer-Johnson Company), simple drawings, words, phrases, or any combination of these.

Order Information for Mayer-Johnson Company

Boardmaker Software (Macintosh and Windows). A communication and learning tool with over 3,000 Picture Communication Symbols (PCS).

Boardmaker Plus! Software. Makes your *Boardmaker* activities talk.

Mayer-Johnson Company
PO Box 1579
Solana Beach, CA 92075

Phone 800/588-4548
Fax 858/550-0449
www.mayer-johnson.com

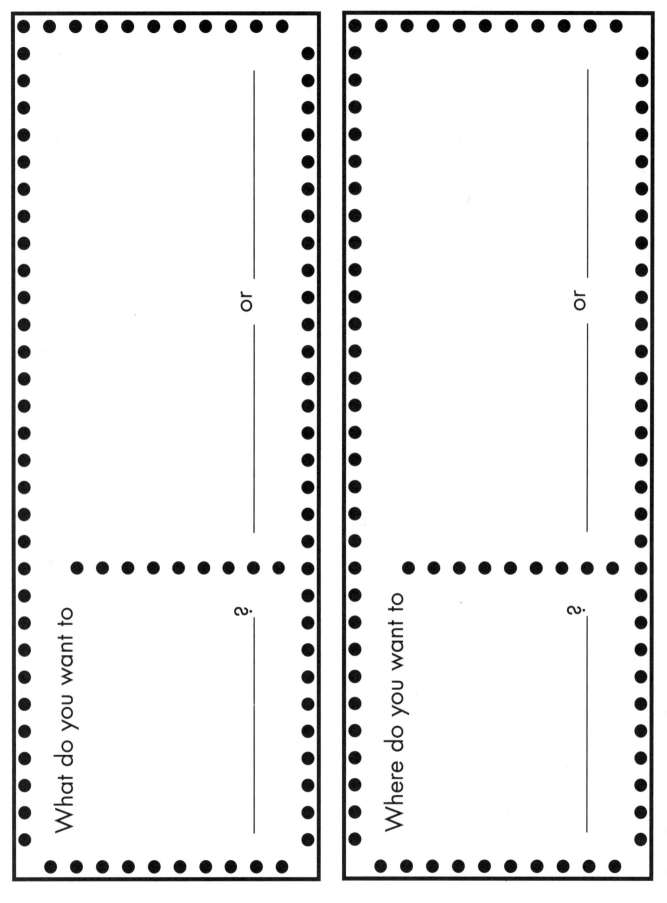

What do you want to _____ ?

_____ or _____

Where do you want to _____ ?

_____ or _____

Idea 23

88

Who do you want to _____ or _____?

When do you want to _____ or _____?

Idea 23

Idea 24
Now–Next Picture Map

Students with autism spectrum disorders often have fewer behavior problems when they have consistent, predictable routines in their lives. Although the consistency can often prevent problems with changes and transitions, too much consistency and sameness may cause another problem, a lack of flexibility or adaptability. Carried to an extreme, this lack of flexibility can result in ritualistic, repetitive, and unproductive behaviors. In order to provide some predictability in situations but still help students adjust, use simple two-part schedules or picture maps.

The Now–Next picture map is a simple tool for helping students transition from one activity to the next. Students should be taught to manage the picture map themselves.

Here's how to use it.

❶ As the student begins an activity, put a picture, symbol, or word on the Now section of the map to indicate what he or she is doing. Attach it with Velcro squares or a similar fastener.

❷ On the right side, attach a representation of what will happen next. Briefly point to each side and indicate what is happening now and what will happen next.

❸ After completing the task or activity at hand, remove the picture, symbol, or word from the Now side, move the Next picture to the left (so it becomes the Now), and add a new representation of what will happen Next. Once again, tell the student what is happening and then prepare him or her for what will happen next.

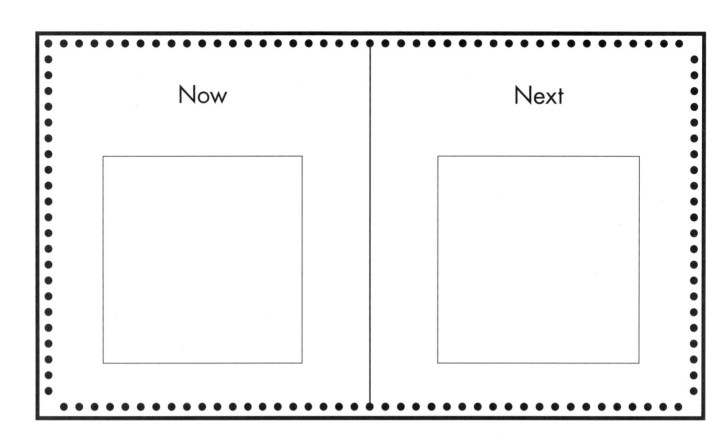

Now | Next

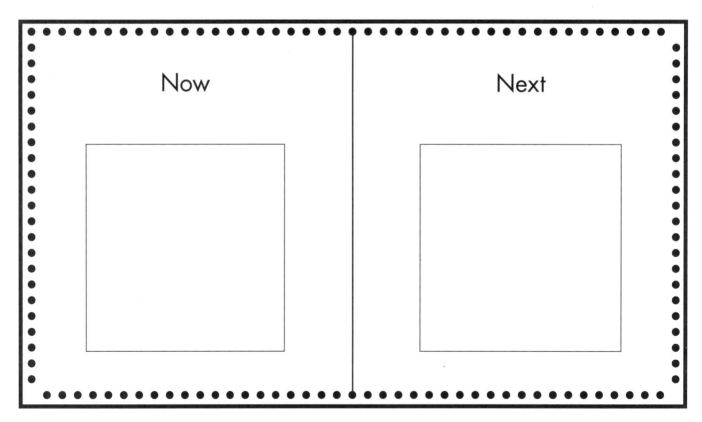

Now | Next

Idea 24

Idea 25
Schedule Changes

Because many students with autism have difficulty when a change in their routines occurs, it is important to have simple, yet effective, methods of communicating those changes. Schedule Changes provide such a format.

Here's how this idea works.

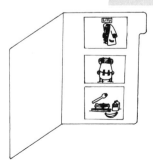

❶ Construct a daily schedule for your student using photographs, icons, symbols, words, objects, or a combination of any of these. Each activity, person, or location the student will encounter during the day should be included. After printing or constructing one small card (2″ × 2″ or a 4″ × 6″ index card size) to represent each item on the schedule, laminate the cards for durability and put Velcro on the back of each if desired. If you are using objects, test them to be sure they cannot be swallowed.

❷ Once you have the individual items for the schedule, select a format that is easy to change, because schedules at school are likely to change often. The schedule should also be easy to handle and hold, since many children with autism have difficulties with fine motor skills or sensitivities related to touch. Options for changeable schedule formats include a

- key ring,
- small photo album,
- card with Velcro squares on which the cards can be attached,
- poster or cardboard strip posted in the classroom,
- file folder with pockets or Velcro squares,
- small strip of poster board with plastic pockets or Velcro squares,
- paper schedule in a clear plastic pocket or taped to a notebook, and a
- tray or open box for younger children who need an object schedule.

❸ Once you have decided on the format of each student's daily schedule, create some additional cards that can be used to cue the student when changes are going to occur. We have provided some called Change Cards. You can use these or create some with your own illustrations or directions. Change Cards can be used in several ways:

- *To cue students first thing in the morning that a change is going to happen that day*

Present the cards individually and talk with the student, showing him or her which changes will occur.

- *To remind students throughout the day that a change will occur*

Insert the change cards directly into the student's schedule, right before the event or person that is going to change from the usual schedule. Refer to the changes often enough to make sure the student gets comfortable with what will happen.

- *As part of the materials used when teaching a social-skills lesson*

Model what to do when a change occurs and use the cards as the signal so that students are prompted to follow a routine when they are agitated or upset. Teach the routine often so that students are familiar with it and can use it almost automatically.

Note. The Change Cards for this idea are from *Practical Ideas That Really Work for Students with Asperger Syndrome* (p. 27), by K. McConnell and G. R. Ryser, 2005, Austin, TX: PRO-ED. Copyright 2005 by PRO-ED, Inc. Reprinted with permission.

**No explosions!
It's just a change.**

**No explosions!
It's just a change.**

**Change is on the way, but
you can handle it.**

**Change is on the way, but
you can handle it.**

Oops! Time for a change.

Oops! Time for a change.

Idea 25

No explosions!

It's just a change.

Change is on the way, but

you can handle it.

Idea 25

Oops!

Time for a change.

No explosions!
It's just a change.

Change is on the way,
but you can handle it.

Oops!
Time for a change.

Idea 25

Idea 26
Learn To Wait

Students with autism often have problems with a key skill: Waiting. Because they find it difficult to wait, transitions from one activity to another may be difficult and behavior problems may arise. We suggest teaching students how to wait and giving them some tools to help them wait without engaging in disruptive or dangerous behaviors.

Here are some key steps in teaching the skill of waiting.

❶ Identify the times of day or situations that require the student to wait. At school, these include situations like waiting in line for lunch, waiting as one activity ends and another begins, and waiting for the bus to go home. At home, waiting for a food at meal time or snack time is often challenging. Plan to teach waiting and then use your planned routine at these challenging times.

❷ Find some age-appropriate activities that are suitable for the student as he or she waits. For example, a student could play with a hand-held game or look at a book while waiting. Locate these items and place them in a portable container.

❸ Teach the behaviors that are acceptable and the behaviors that are not acceptable during waiting. Acceptable behaviors might include sitting and playing with a squeeze ball or listening to music on headphones, whatever you identified in Step 2. Unacceptable behaviors include running around, grabbing things, or screaming. One of the easiest and clearest ways to identify the behaviors that you want to see during waiting is to use a T chart that helps identify what you want to see and what you want to hear (see example on next page). The behaviors you want to see and hear will depend on the situation, the student's age, your own tolerance for specific behaviors, and other variables. Anything not on the T-chart is inappropriate.

❹ Create a cue card for waiting. We have provided an example that is based on the T-chart example. Use photographs, picture symbols, words, or a combination of these. The cue card will remind the student what waiting looks like and sounds like and also what not to do. Our examples include all of those elements.

❺ To make sure the student learns the process, model, guide, review, practice numerous times as part of instruction, and then provide lots of positive reinforcement. To help students improve their waiting skills by waiting appropriately for longer periods of time, we suggest using an inexpensive sand timer. Many school supply stores sell these timers, which usually last for intervals of 1, 2, 3, or 5 minutes. There are several Web sites for game materials that also sell the sand timers. We suggest using a series of timers as you teach this skill. For example, first use the 1-minute timer, then the 3-minute timer, and finally the 5-minute timer. These timers are great visual reminders for both students and adults. The timers are small, portable, and easy to understand, all important characteristics when teaching students with autism to wait.

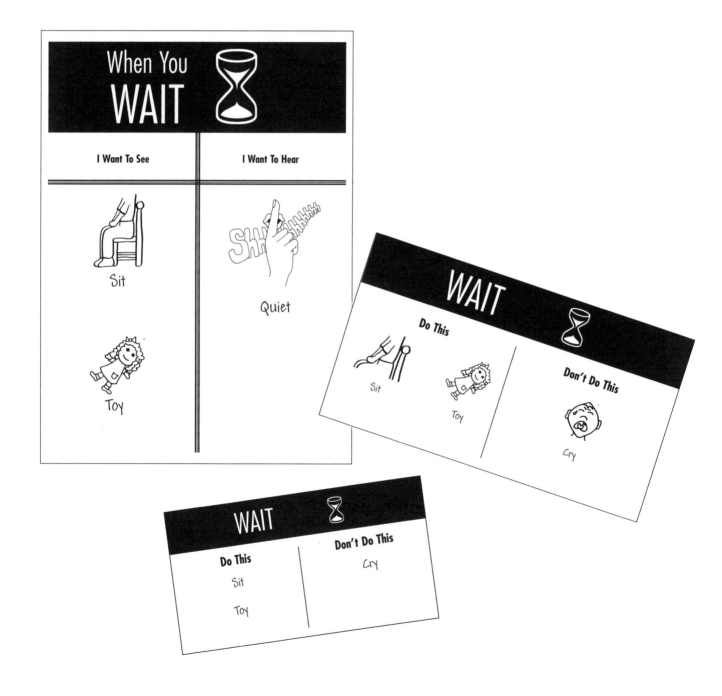

When You WAIT

I Want To See

I Want To Hear

Idea 26

WAIT

Do This | **Don't Do This**

WAIT

Do This | **Don't Do This**

WAIT

Do This | **Don't Do This**

Idea 26

Idea 27
Teaching Independence

It can be very difficult to teach students with autism spectrum disorders to complete actions or demonstrate behaviors independently. Despite the best efforts of educators, therapists, parents, or other caregivers, students often remain dependent on cues or prompts, fail to initiate actions, or require high levels of guidance and supervision. Independence is more important as students get older, so helping them learn to act independently is critical.

Routines can be useful when teaching independent behavior. Instructing students in routines can involve many steps and may require many decisions. We have tried to simplify this process by designing a straightforward model called Teaching Independence. This practical strategy can address many goals and objectives related to independent behavior.

Here's how it works.

❶ Decide on the routine that you would like to teach, and write it at the top of the Teaching Independence form. We suggest that you select a routine that occurs regularly in the student's day or week. A list of common school routines that students can learn to do independently is provided in the Typical School Routines form. This form can also be used to evaluate the student's level of performance on the specific routines. In our example, we have chosen to teach Jenny the skill of "stopping an activity."

❷ Decide on the steps of the routine. These steps should be stated behaviorally (i.e., as a description of exactly what you would like to see and hear the student do). Begin with a simple routine—one with three or fewer steps. These steps are what you will model for the student. Write the steps in the first column of the Teaching Independence form. In our example, the three steps we would like to see and hear are:

1. Say, "I'm stopping."

2. Put materials away.

3. Sit and wait for the next direction.

Note. The Typical School Routines form is from *Early Start for Young Children with Autism/PDD: Practical Interventions* (p. 93), by K. McConnell and G. R. Ryser, Illustrations by J. Loehr, 2006, Austin, TX: PRO-ED. Copyright 2006 by PRO-ED, Inc. Reprinted with permission.

If there are required prerequisite skills or routines that have not been taught, you may need to go back and teach those first. For example, waiting is a key skill for many students, and you may have a specific routine that you want to see for appropriate waiting. If the student does not know how to wait, that routine may take precedence over stopping an activity.

❸ The next component of teaching the routine is to choose the words that you will say as directions for each step. Directions should be short, direct, and clear. Writing them on the form, in the second column, will help everyone who works with the student remain consistent. The same words should be used each time the routine is taught. In our example, we decided on these verbal directions:

1. "Jenny, please say, 'I'm stopping.'"

2. "Jenny, please put your materials away."

3. "Jenny, please sit and wait."

❹ Once you know what the steps to the routine are and have decided on visual cues and verbal directions, it is time to begin to teach. As you model the routine, give your verbal directions, and use appropriate cues and prompts to ensure that the student is following through. In the third column on the form, write the date that you introduce the routine. Each time you practice it after that, write the practice dates. Please note that some routines take a very long time to teach. You may want to photocopy the form after completing the first two columns so that you have adequate recording space. In our example, we are going to teach the routine two times each day. We began on January 11, 2006, and practiced two times the next day, January 12, 2006.

❺ In the last column of the form, you can record the student's progress. Circle "yes" if he or she demonstrated the step, and circle "no" if not. Also circle "Ph" if you used physical assistance, "Vis" for a visual prompt, and "Ver" if you gave the direction verbally. You may need to use all three of these or none of these. In our example, we began by using a visual and verbal directions for Step 1, all three types of assistance for Step 2, and only a verbal direction for Step 3.

❻ Each time the student demonstrates any or all steps in the routine, provide positive reinforcement. Many options for reinforcement are provided in Idea 37, Positive Reinforcement.

❼ Reduce prompting. Effective methods for reducing your level of prompting are provided in Idea 31, Reduce Prompts.

Teaching Independence

Name __Jenny__   Routine __Stopping an activity__

STEPS	WORDS	PRACTICE	PROGRESS				
❶ Say, "I'm stopping."	Jenny, please say, "I'm stopping."	Introduction Date __Jan. 11, 2006__	Yes	(No)	Ph	(Vis)	(Ver)
		Practice Dates					
		__Jan. 12__	Yes	(No)	Ph	(Vis)	(Ver)
		__Jan. 12__	(Yes)	No	Ph	(Vis)	(Ver)
		_____	Yes	No	Ph	Vis	Ver
		_____	Yes	No	Ph	Vis	Ver
		_____	Yes	No	Ph	Vis	Ver
❷ Put materials away.	Jenny, please put your materials away.	Introduction Date __Jan. 11, 2006__	Yes	(No)	(Ph)	(Vis)	(Ver)
		Practice Dates					
		__Jan. 12__	Yes	(No)	(Ph)	(Vis)	(Ver)
		__Jan. 12__	Yes	(No)	(Ph)	(Vis)	(Ver)
		_____	Yes	No	Ph	Vis	Ver
		_____	Yes	No	Ph	Vis	Ver
		_____	Yes	No	Ph	Vis	Ver
❸ Sit and wait for the next direction.	Jenny, please sit and wait.	Introduction Date __Jan. 11, 2006__	Yes	(No)	Ph	Vis	(Ver)
		Practice Dates					
		__Jan. 12__	(Yes)	No	Ph	Vis	(Ver)
		__Jan. 12__	(Yes)	No	Ph	Vis	Ver
		_____	Yes	No	Ph	Vis	Ver
		_____	Yes	No	Ph	Vis	Ver
		_____	Yes	No	Ph	Vis	Ver

Typical School Routines

Name _____

Date _____

	Cannot Do It	Needs Much Help	Needs Little Help	Can Do It
• Getting on the bus or in the car				
• Getting off the bus or out of the car				
• Greeting adults				
• Entering school				
• Entering the classroom				
• Hanging up coat and backpack				
• Greeting classmates and adults				
• Sitting down				
• Checking calendar or schedule				
• Getting ready to work in small group				
• Getting ready to work alone				
• Waiting				
• Asking for help				
• Starting a new activity				
• Stopping an activity				
• Moving from one place to another in school				
• Entering and leaving classrooms				
• Getting ready for a snack				
• Entering and leaving the cafeteria				
• Having lunch				
• Picking up materials				
• Getting ready to go home				
• Walking to the bus or car				
• Saying good-bye				

Idea 27

Teaching Independence

Name _____   Routine _____

STEPS	WORDS	PRACTICE	PROGRESS				
❶		Introduction Date _____	Yes	No	Ph	Vis	Ver
		Practice Dates _____	Yes	No	Ph	Vis	Ver
		_____	Yes	No	Ph	Vis	Ver
		_____	Yes	No	Ph	Vis	Ver
		_____	Yes	No	Ph	Vis	Ver
		_____	Yes	No	Ph	Vis	Ver
❷		Introduction Date _____	Yes	No	Ph	Vis	Ver
		Practice Dates _____	Yes	No	Ph	Vis	Ver
		_____	Yes	No	Ph	Vis	Ver
		_____	Yes	No	Ph	Vis	Ver
		_____	Yes	No	Ph	Vis	Ver
		_____	Yes	No	Ph	Vis	Ver
❸		Introduction Date _____	Yes	No	Ph	Vis	Ver
		Practice Dates _____	Yes	No	Ph	Vis	Ver
		_____	Yes	No	Ph	Vis	Ver
		_____	Yes	No	Ph	Vis	Ver
		_____	Yes	No	Ph	Vis	Ver
		_____	Yes	No	Ph	Vis	Ver

Idea 27

Idea 28

Do More To Learn More

Students with autism spectrum disorders are often taught a two-step routine using a visual format of completing an assignment and earning a preferred activity or object. This procedure establishes a very important contingency for students: First you have to work, then you get something you like. However, teachers, parents, and therapists should continually raise their expectations for performance and not to stick indefinitely with a routine that requires only one task before earning positive reinforcement. Only if students with autism spectrum disorders are expected to do more will they learn more. Do More To Learn More is easy to use and can be modified as necessary. There are two forms provided to help you implement this idea, the I Choose form and the I Am Working form.

Here are the steps for using this strategy.

❶ Ask the student to make a choice of a preferred activity, object, or other positive reinforcer. (For reinforcement suggestions, see Idea 37, Positive Reinforcement.) When first teaching students to make choices, present only two options. The choices can be presented as objects, photographs, picture symbols, or in print, depending on the student's communication style, on the I Choose form.

❷ Decide on the number of assignments the student must complete. The number of assignments for completion should be challenging to the student but not overwhelming. For example, if Hank has been completing only one task before receiving positive reinforcement, increase the requirement to two; if Hank typically completes two assignments before an activity of his choice, increase the requirement to three. On the I Am Working form, we have provided three rows for reinforcement after completing three, four, or five assignments, respectively.

 Tip:

For more information on how to communicate what each assignment entails, see Idea 30, Five Ways To Finish.

3. Present the student's assignments one at a time. All assignments should be taught according to a lesson plan that has been specifically designed for him or her. As the student completes each assignment, place a check mark, stamp, sticker, smiley face, or other symbol in the box on the I Am Working form. Hank loves baseball, so we put a baseball sticker in the box after he completes each assignment.

4. After the student has completed the required tasks, he or she can begin to enjoy the preferred activity chosen. It is usually best to decide ahead of time how long to let the student engage in the preferred activity and to signal the end of his time with a timer. We let Hank look at baseball magazines for 4 minutes and when the timer sounds, he gets back to work.

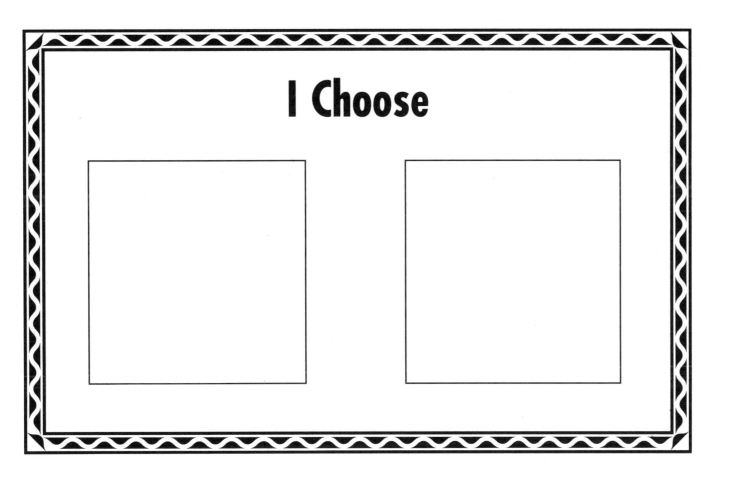

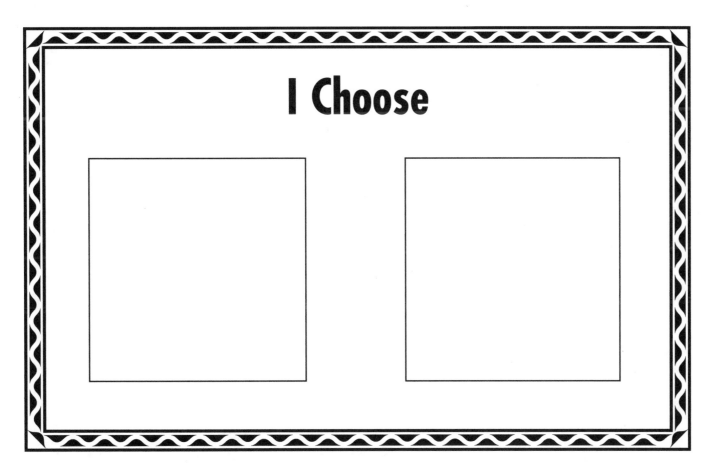

Idea 28

I Am Working

I will finish _____ assignments.

Each time I finish, I will get

Idea 28

Idea 29
On Your Own

Maintaining consistent attention to task and working independently are two related skills that are often difficult to teach students with autism. There are many reasons why independent work and attention to task can be a challenge, including students' distractibility, their dependence on prompts and cues, and the difficulty of the task. On Your Own is a highly structured approach to independent work for students with autism. It involves a visual format, the use of a timer, a preferred activity used as positive reinforcement, and a token system. On Your Own also includes immediate positive reinforcement for each minute that the student is working independently. In the beginning, this strategy requires constant attention and monitoring from an adult; however, that attention should gradually be reduced as soon as possible.

Here's how to implement On Your Own.

❶ Decide on the task you would like the student to complete independently, and estimate how long the task should take. Choose a simple task at first, one you feel sure that the student can complete on his or her own.

❷ For each minute you estimate the task will require, place one token on the top of the On Your Own card. We have provided a template for this card and a master for the tokens. The first template has space for 10 tokens, indicating a goal of 10 minutes of independent work. If the student masters that goal, you can use the second template, which has space for 20 tokens. When a student reaches the goal of 20 minutes of independent work, you should be reducing your level of supervision and reinforcement. In our example, we want Vivian to complete a math activity that should take approximately 6 minutes, so we place six tokens at the top of her card.

❸ Place a picture, symbol, or words representing the student's preferred activity or choice that is being used as a positive reinforcer on the left side of the card. For example, Vivian loves to listen to music, so we used the word, "Music" and a picture of her favorite CD.

> ### 🧩 Tip:
> You can use coins, poker chips, or other tokens that you already have instead of the tokens we have provided.

④ Under the preferred activity, there are outlines for the tokens. Draw a vertical line after the number representing the minutes you are allowing for the task. In our example, we have drawn a line after six tokens because Vivian has to work for 6 minutes to earn her activity.

⑤ Provide directions for the student's assignment and, if necessary, model it so that the task requirements are clear. Remind the student that he or she will earn one token and 1 minute of activity time for each minute he or she stays on task. Then tell the student to begin. In our case, we will show Vivian how to do the first math activity, do one problem with her, and then direct her to begin the work independently.

⑥ Set the timer for 1 minute (we recommend against using a wind-up kitchen timer, because the ticking is often distracting to students with autism. Instead, use a small digital or a visual timer). When the timer sounds at the end of 1 minute, make a judgment regarding the student's level of independent work.

- If the student has worked consistently for the minute, he or she earns a token representing a minute of preferred activity time. Remove a token from the top of the card and place it under the picture of the preferred activity. Explain or show that this is 1 minute of activity time. Also provide enthusiastic verbal praise for working hard. For example, Vivian works well for the first minute, earns a token, and places it under the music picture herself.

- If the student has not worked for the minute time period, take one token from the top of the page and put it in the Time Lost envelope. This represents activity time that the student will not receive. As you place the token in the envelope, explain as simply as possible that this time has been lost because he or she did not work hard. (Use simple words like "no time," "time lost," or "time lost this time, work hard next time." Point to the Time Lost envelope, and also point to the activity to remind the student what he or she can earn.)

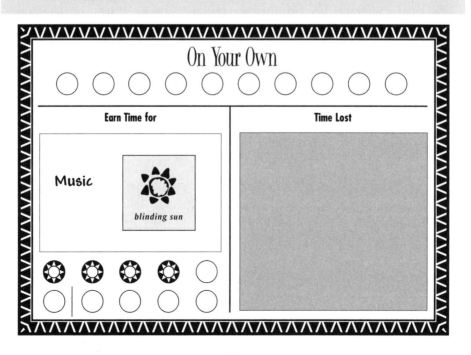

7 Repeat the process for each minute you have estimated necessary for completion of the independent work. In our example, Vivian worked during 4 of her 6 minutes, so she has four tokens, representing 4 minutes of activity time.

8 Immediately after the work time is over, count the number of tokens aloud with the student, explaining how much time he or she has earned, and then set the timer, or allow the student to set the timer, for the same amount of time. Allow the student access to the activity he or she has selected. When the timer goes off, the student should put his or her preferred activity away and get back to work.

9 Repeat the process often and until the student has improved his or her time spent in independent work. Record the student's progress on the Duration Chart provided. Review his or her progress weekly, then make necessary changes to the program based on this progress.

Helpful Hints

- As soon as the student is working independently for short time periods, gradually increase the total amount of time he or she must work to earn a preferred activity. For example, if you have required only 3 minutes of work for a student, increase to 5 minutes of required work to earn an activity.

- After a period of successful independent work, change the ratio of work to activity time. For example, 2 minutes of independent work = 1 minute of a preferred activity.

- Gradually increase the time intervals between reinforcement. For example, check on the student every 2 minutes instead of each minute.

- Decrease your physical proximity to the student. Instead of standing or sitting close to him or her, move further away so that you can still evaluate the performance. You want the student to focus on his or her own performance and not become dependent on your presence as a reminder to work.

On Your Own

Time Lost

Earn Time for

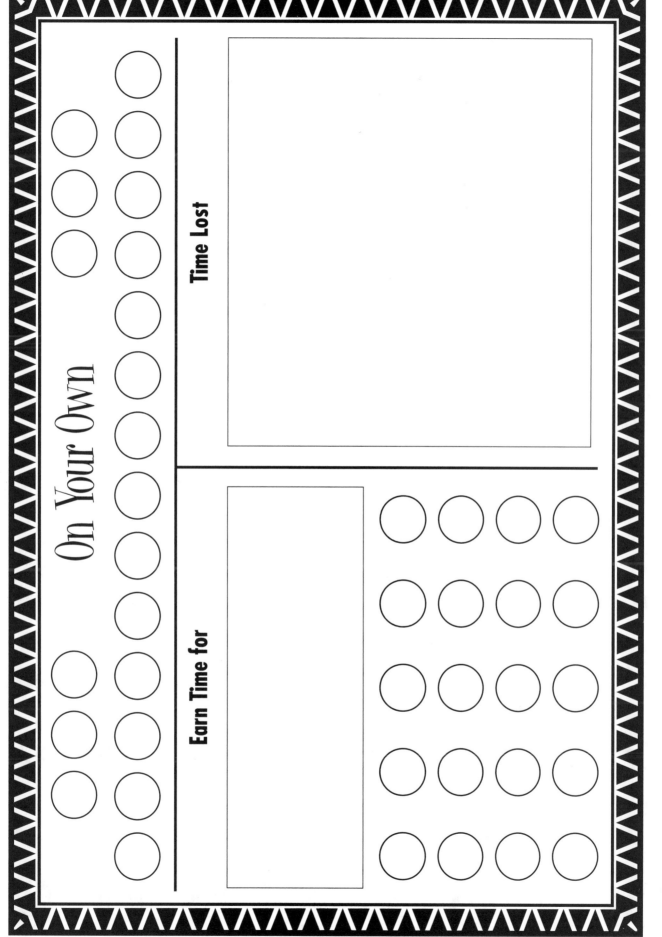

On Your Own

Time Lost

Earn Time for

117

Time Lost Pocket Template

Cut out the pocket on the solid lines, and fold on the dotted lines. Place glue on the outer folds and attach to the Time for Work card.

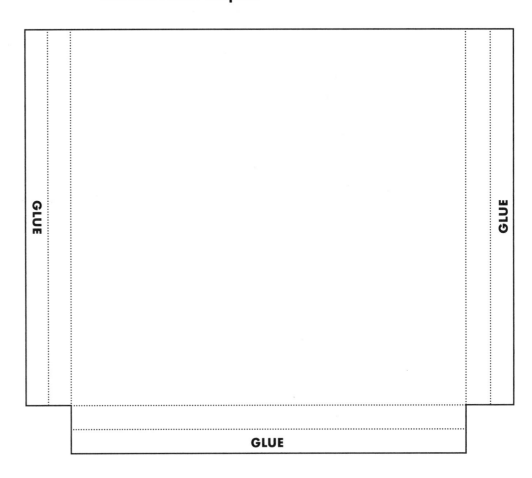

Tokens

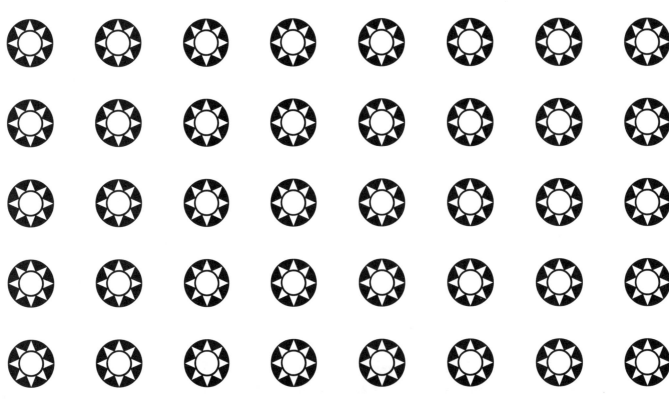

Idea 29

Duration Chart

Name: _____ Date: _____

Behavior: _____

Trials _____

1	Stop Time	_____ : _____
	Start Time	_____ : _____
	Duration	_____ : _____

2	Stop Time	_____ : _____
	Start Time	_____ : _____
	Duration	_____ : _____

3	Stop Time	_____ : _____
	Start Time	_____ : _____
	Duration	_____ : _____

4	Stop Time	_____ : _____
	Start Time	_____ : _____
	Duration	_____ : _____

5	Stop Time	_____ : _____
	Start Time	_____ : _____
	Duration	_____ : _____

Average Duration _____ : _____

Idea 29

Idea 30
Five Ways To Finish

Students with autism spectrum disorders usually require a highly organized environment that includes a work system to manage assignments. Decisions about work systems within the environment should address many factors, especially those relevant to an individual student's strengths, limitations, style of learning, communication abilities, and behavioral history. The decisions often include the following:

- How to signal the beginning and end of the activity (e.g., a timer or bell)

- How long the student has to work if sustained work is the goal (e.g., 10 minutes for a young child and a half hour for an older student)

- How much work must be completed (e.g., five repetitions of an action or three completed matching cards)

- The conditions of the task (with or without assistance)

- The criteria for success (all answers must be correct, or with new learning, 25% must be correct)

- The location where the assignment should be completed (the student must sit at an individual desk or work at a table with others)

- How to help the student understand what he or she must do to be finished (e.g., complete what is in two folders, not the whole stack of folders)

A basic but important step in communicating work expectations to students with autism is to provide a method of separating unfinished from finished work. This separation can clearly communicate to the student what he or she must do and when he or she is done. Without this understanding, many students resist assignments, refusing to start, stick with the task, or finish. Teaching a student when he or she is finished can help build a routine and prevent misbehavior. This idea provides ways to separate unfinished from finished work and to indicate to student when he or she is "finished."

🐚 Tips:

- ⊙ Use color coding (e.g., students' math work is always in the red folder, language arts is always in the green folder, and science work is always in the yellow folder).

- ⊙ Don't forget that in addition to environmental organization that tells the student when work is completed, most students will also need a visual or auditory signal or a physical or verbal cue.

Here are five ways to finish.

❶ *Use a pocket folder.* Put unfinished work in the pocket on the left side and finished work in the pocket on the right side. As work is moved from left to right, the student can see what is completed and what is left to do. Label each side by placing a photo, symbol, or word on the pocket.

❷ *Use plastic tubs.* For students who are working with manipulatives, clear plastic tubs are great. Simply put all the materials for one assignment in the tub. The student will be expected to complete whatever is in that tub when it is presented. When you present the work tub, also present an empty tub with a "finished" label. As the student completes each part of the assignment, put it in the finished tub. The student will know that he or she is through working when the work tub is empty and the finished tub is full. Afterwards, dump the materials back into the work tub, put the lid on it, and return it to its shelf.

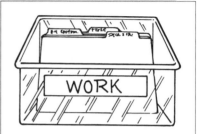
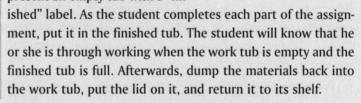
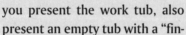

❸ *Use a tray with Velcro pieces or strips attached to the bottom of the tray.* To use this approach, present the tray with objects attached and also present an empty box or tray marked "finished." Remove the items from the Velcro one at a time, complete the assigned task, and then place them on the finished tray or in the finished box. Use this method with young students or students with motor impairments. Activities like matching two items, arranging items from small to big, or putting letters in alphabetical order are easily organized on a tray.

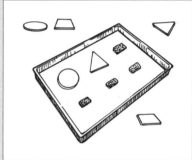
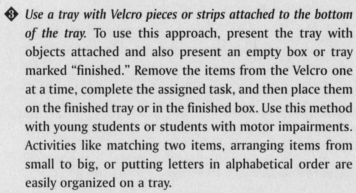

❹ *Attach heavy, stiff fabric envelopes or pouches to the sides of the student's desk.* This method works well when you want students to remain seated. The student can take unfinished work from the envelope on one side of the desk and then when completed, place it in the envelope on the other side of the desk. This type of envelope or pouch is easy to sew or can be constructed by hot gluing fabric onto a cardboard envelope.

❺ *Use letter trays, cardboard boxes with low sides, or baskets.* Many office supply stores have attractive and inexpensive items, and garage sales and flea markets often have used office items for sale. The key to using these items effectively for students with autism is to label them clearly (often with both a written word and a photograph or picture symbol) and then use them consistently. Students should be directed to get their work from the same place each time they begin, work in the same location, and then place completed work in the same container. This will build an effective work routine.

Idea 31
Reduce Prompts

Although instruction in routines can be simple, especially using the model in Idea 27, Teaching Independence, some methods of insuring that the student begins to complete the routine independently are necessary. Otherwise, you might find yourself using prompts, cues, or assistance long after beginning to teach. Following are several strategies to help you reduce your assistance and build your student's independent actions:

- **After a step in the routine, wait.** Do not move to the next step immediately. Waiting gives the student the opportunity to perform the next step without your instruction or assistance.

- **Use an unobtrusive cue, like a glance.** While still a cue, your "look" is much less assistance than a verbal direction or a physical prompt. It can also be eliminated much more easily when you think the student no longer requires it.

- **Ask a question.** After any step in a routine, you can look confused and ask the student what to do. Say something simple like "What's next?" or ask "What should you do?" Of course, wait while you see if you get an appropriate response.

- **Keep visual cues accessible and visible.** Although you may want to eventually eliminate all cues, even visuals, keeping them around while the student is still mastering the routine can be just what he or she needs. Students can often look at visuals and follow the indicated steps without any further prompting or directions.

- **Include other students in the routine.** Adults are not the only models students look to for cues on how to behave. Including other students in a routine may encourage a student to learn it more quickly and to follow the routine without adult interference.

- **Use structure to encourage routine completion.** Use a reinforcing activity after routine completion. This is a powerful tool in helping students independently complete their routines.

Idea 32
Door Signs

Some students with an autism spectrum disorder demonstrate behaviors that are dangerous and that put them at risk for harm. One such behavior is leaving a classroom or area without permission, which sometimes includes running away from adults. Door Signs is a simple idea that will help you communicate to students, especially very young children, that they are not to leave an area.

To use door signs, create a sign that indicates that leaving the room without permission is not allowed. Following are some examples:

- Take a picture of the student with his or her hand on the door knob, about to open the door. On top of the picture, draw a large red universal "no" sign (circle with a slash in the middle).

- For students who can read, make a sign that says, "No Leaving" in large letters.

- Use a picture symbol that shows someone running away and put the universal "no" sign on it, or put the word "NO" in front of the picture in large, red letters.

The format that you use should match the communication style and age of the student. We have provided some examples and a frame that hints at the sign's purpose. Once you have created the sign, place the sign at the student's eye level, next to the door knob. Refer to the sign several times each day, using the sign as a teaching tool and as a reminder. Explain to the student that he or she is not to leave the classroom without permission.

To make this idea even more effective, you can combine it with a system of positive reinforcement: Each hour (or morning, afternoon, day) that the student stays in the room, he or she earns a poker chip, sticker, or penny. When the student accumulates 10 of these, he or she can have 10 minutes of uninterrupted time to engage in a preferred activity.

125

Idea 32

Idea 32

128

Idea 32

Idea 33
Four-Step Behavior Plan

Many approaches to behavior management of students with autism spectrum disorders are focused on reducing or eliminating behaviors. These students often demonstrate behaviors that are inappropriate, disruptive, dangerous, or only unacceptable in specific situations—just reducing or eliminating those behaviors does not teach the student what he or she should do instead.

The Four-Step Behavior Plan is a simple and straightforward way to teach replacement behaviors. The plan is designed for use with students of almost any age, and if it is reproduced in a durable format, it can be used in all settings. When you use the Four-Step Behavior Plan, consider using both visuals and words. Students may be agitated or upset at the time when the plan is needed the most, and visuals may help them process and understand information more easily.

To use the plan, follow these steps.

❶ Identify the behavior that you would like to reduce or eliminate. Pick one behavior at a time. Next, put a picture, drawing, or photograph of that behavior in the first box on the form. On top of that picture, put the universal "no" sign or an X. Use a thick red or black line so that the student understands that the behavior is not acceptable. In our example, we would like Jorgé to stop running away. In the first box on the form, we have put a picture of Jorgé running. On top of that picture we have put the universal "no" sign. We have also written the words, "No Running Away." When we teach Jorgé to follow the four part plan, we will show him the picture many times and repeat, "No running away."

❷ In the second box, place a visual and the corresponding words that tell the student what you *do* want him or her to do. This is the important replacement behavior. Without your instruction and reinforcement, many students will find their own replacement behaviors, which may not be acceptable either. Again, use a visual and a word or short phrase. In our example, we put a picture of Jorgé sitting and waiting. We also put the words, "Sit and Wait."

> **🌀 Tip:**
>
> To get maximum results, always try to use a behavior in Box 2 that is incompatible with the behavior in Box 1. This will help the student learn faster and ensure that any replacement behaviors are behaviors that are acceptable and positive.

3 In the third box on the form, show the criteria or standard that the student must meet. For example, how many times, how long, or under what circumstances the replacement behavior must be demonstrated. In our example, we want Jorgé to sit and wait instead of running away after at least five activities that occur during the morning. Consequently, we have put the numbers 1 through 5 in this box. Each time Jorgé finishes something in class, and instead of running away, sits and waits, we will cross off a number. After he has done this five times, he will have earned an activity. You could use a clock with a specific amount of time showing, a number representing minutes, a picture of a student working alone instead of with assistance, or any other relevant picture for Box 3.

4 Finally, in the last box, put a picture of the item or activity that the student will earn by demonstrating the second behavior and not demonstrating the first behavior. Use words and a visual whenever possible. For Jorgé, who loves to take walks, we have put a picture of him taking a walk and the word, "Walk."

Four-Step Behavior Plan

No This	Do This	This Long/Many	To Earn
No Running Away	Sit and Wait	1 2 3 4 5	Walk

Four-Step Behavior Plan

No This	Do This	This Long/Many	To Earn

Idea 34
Social Skills in Pictures

There are many effective and straightforward ways to teach social skills with pictures or other visuals. Use simple drawings, photos, or have students create their own drawings. Following are two formats that should help create social skills materials for everyday use: cartoons and stories. If you would like additional suggestions for using pictures to support students as they learn, practice, and demonstrate specific social skills, you can also refer to other ideas in the manual: Show Me, The Daily Scoop, Now–Next Picture Map, and Schedule Changes.

Here are ways to use cartoons and stories.

❶ Cartoons (three different forms, pp. 136–138)

- One-, two-, or three-frame cartoons are very useful in helping students understand what to do in specific social situations. You can organize the cartoons however you like to deal with a variety of situations or teaching styles.

- One-frame cartoons can be used as reminders or cues. For example, a picture of the student listening while another student is talking can be used as a reminder not to monopolize a conversation.

- With a two-frame cartoon, you can use the first frame to draw a problem and the second frame to show a solution. For example, when a student is teased, one response might be to ignore the teasing. So Step 1 of the cartoon shows the student being teased, and Step 2 shows the student walking away.

someone teases me
Problem

walk away
Solution

Note. This idea is from *Practical Ideas That Really Work for Students with Asperger Syndrome* (pp. 107–117), by K. McConnell and G. R. Ryser, 2005, Austin, TX: PRO-ED. Copyright 2005 by PRO-ED, Inc. Reprinted with permission.

133

- If the student is facing a complicated situation, then the three-frame cartoon might be best. You can show three steps for dealing with the problem. For example, if a student has forgotten his lunch, he can (1) tell the teacher and ask permission to call home or ask someone in the office to call home, (2) pick up his lunch from the office if someone can bring it, or (3) borrow money from the office or cafeteria if the lunch cannot be delivered to school.

- The cartoon frames can be titled, labeled, put in a notebook, or posted in the student's work area—whatever meets the student's needs.

❷ Stories (three different forms, pp. 139–143)

- Stories used to teach social skills are very common and can be reproduced from commercial materials, constructed by a teacher, or created by the student. When creating the stories, it is best to use a minimum of words and a lot of pictures. This will help students who remember what they see, do not process language well when upset, or have problems either talking too much or talking too little in difficult situations. Picture stories for social skills instruction can be designed to fit each individual student's needs.

- Full-page formats are great for younger students. We recommend that you involve the students in the drawing, either by asking them to draw themselves in a situation or by helping you by pointing out details for the drawing. The pages can present the problem and then present a solution, using a single page or a simple two-page format. For example, if a student needs help opening her locker, the first page can show her in front of the locker looking frustrated. The second page can show her asking a teacher for help.

- Smaller, multiple-page or multiple-step books can also be used. However, it is important to avoid very complicated, involved scenarios or solutions. If the visuals have too much information, they may confuse rather than simplify the process. The example provided is for a student who needs to learn to calm himself down. The first page simply says "Chill Out" and shows an ice cube, which is the student's visual cue to begin the calming-down process.

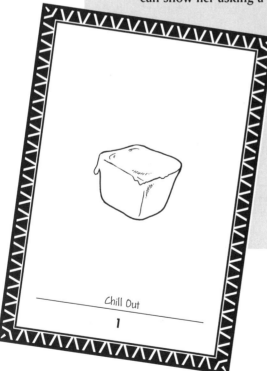

Chill Out

1

The second page shows the first option—taking deep breaths. The third page shows the other option—leaving the classroom and going to the counselor's office for a few minutes. The last page shows the student returning calmly to the classroom. This format is good for older students, who may need more than one choice for solving a social problem. The form provided should be copied on the front and back of a piece of paper, cut out, then folded down the center to create a four-page book.

Take Deep Breaths

2

Ms. Bishop
Counselor

Go to Counselor's Office

3

Calmly Return to Class

4

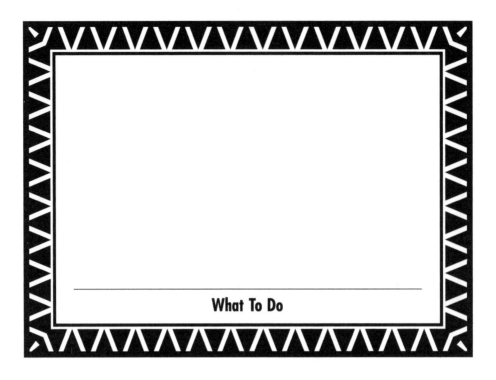

What To Do

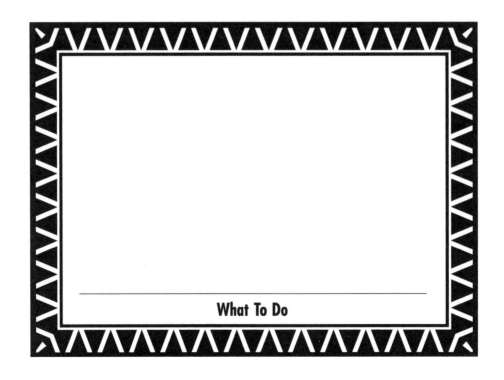

What To Do

Idea 34

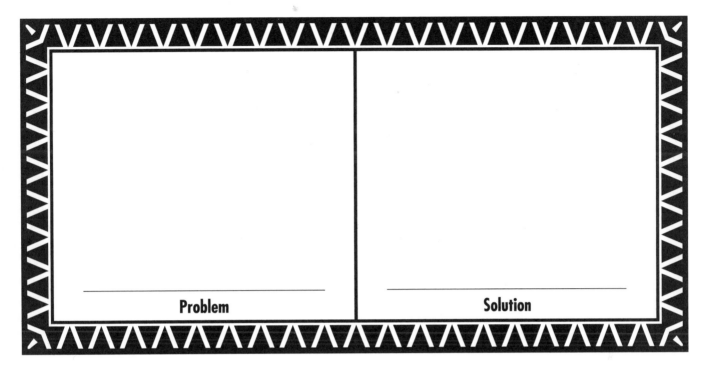

Problem   Solution

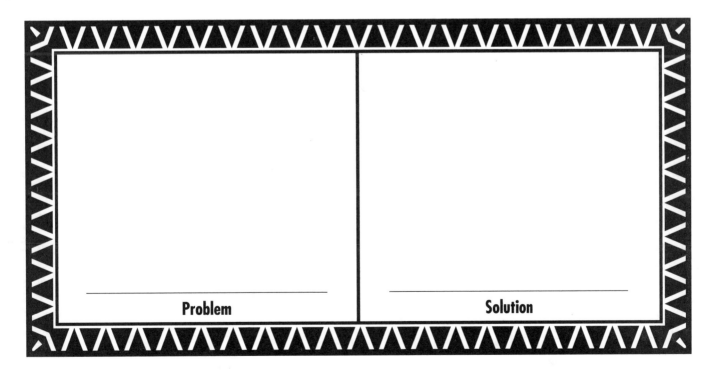

Problem   Solution

Idea 34

Cartoons

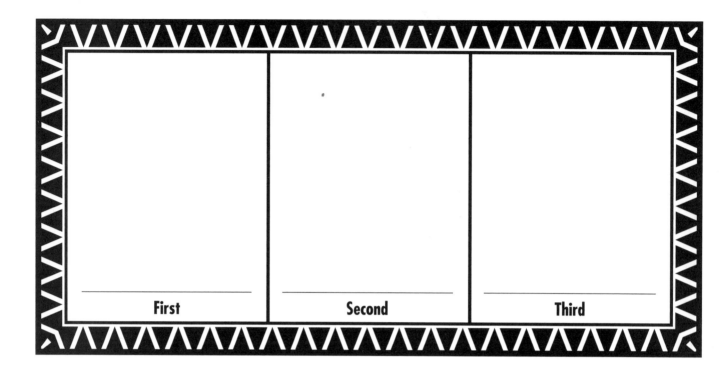

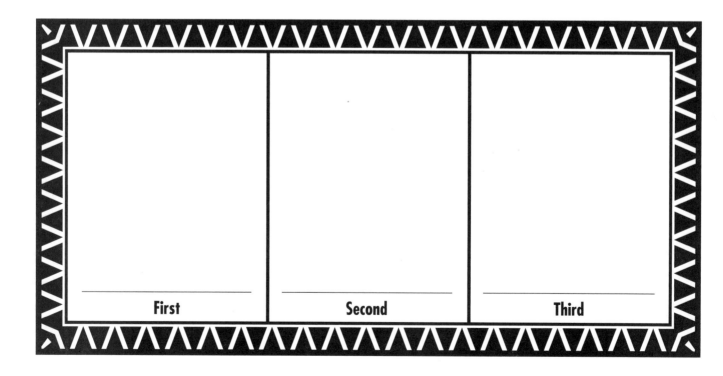

138

Idea 34

What I Will Do When

_____

Idea 34

This Is Hard for Me

_____

1

Idea 34

This Is What I Can Do

2

Idea 34

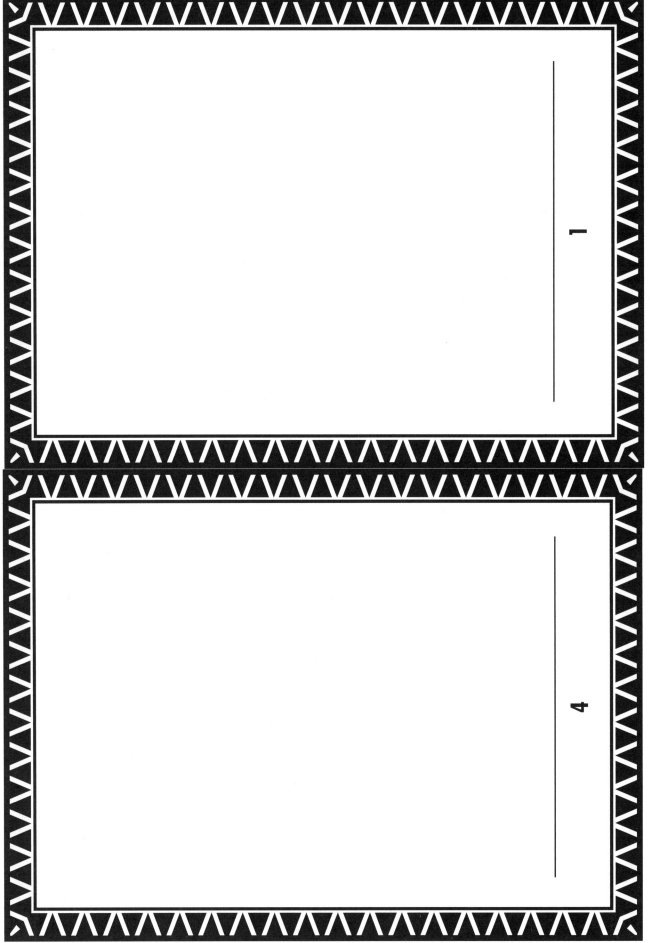

1

4

3

2

Idea 35
Use Video Modeling

Video modeling is an effective strategy for teaching social responses and other behaviors to students with autism spectrum disorders. In video modeling, children view a video featuring peers or familiar adults performing the targeted behavior.

Here's how it works.

❶ Choose the target behavior.

❷ Prepare several video segments, 1 to 5 minutes in length, of peers or familiar adults performing the behavior.

❸ Show the child the video segments, one at a time, across a period of several days.

Variations that can be incorporated include the following:

- Use video self-modeling, a strategy in which the child views videotapes of him- or herself performing the targeted behavior.

- Use prompts, either from teachers or peers, to elicit the desired behavior.

- Embed explicit instructions for the target behavior in the video.

- Use a self-management technique, such as a schedule, to provide for generalization.

Example for Making Requests

❶ Prepare several video segments using an orchestrated play sequence in which two peers are playing a game, playing with play dough, and playing with a favorite toy. Have the peers make several types of requests, such as, "May I have some play dough?" "May I take my turn now?"

❷ Show one of the video segments to the child each day for 5 consecutive days.

❸ Prompt the child during play to make a request, gradually withdrawing the prompts.

❹ Use the reinforcement checklist provided. Make sure to model how to use it by showing the student the checklist, making a request, and marking off one box. Then say, "When you make two requests, you get a prize."

 Tip:

Copy the checklist, write the desired behavior at the top, copy one of the reward icons provided in the Appendix into the bottom box, and laminate.

Make Requests

Make Requests

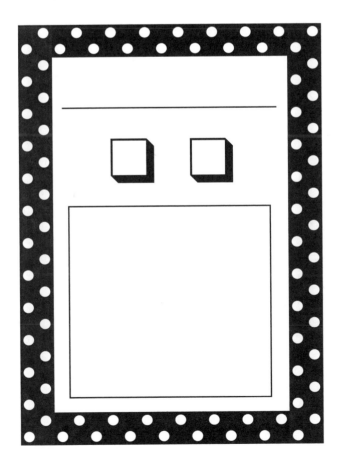

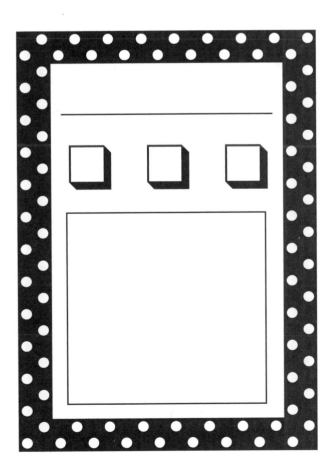

147

Idea 35

Idea 36
Card Counters

When teaching new behaviors to students with an autism spectrum disorder, it is often a good idea to use a system of positive reinforcement that is concrete, visual, and easy to manage. Card Counters are a great way to ensure all three of these characteristics, and they can be used to record and reinforce students each time they demonstrate a target behavior. To use the cards, set a goal with the student, then punch with a hole punch, color in with a marker, or cover the holes with small stickers after each occurrence of the target behavior. Students enjoy seeing their progress, and you have a simple management and reinforcement system.

There are endless possibilities to fit the age and interests of all students. We have provided examples to get you started, but use your imagination, and also let your students help with ideas.

Note. The butterfly forms for this idea are from *Early Start for Young Children with Autism/PDD: Practical Interventions* (pp. 164–165), by K. McConnell and G. R. Ryser, Illustrations by J. Loehr, 2006, Austin, TX: PRO-ED. Copyright 2006 by PRO-ED, Inc. Reprinted with permission.

150

Idea 36

151

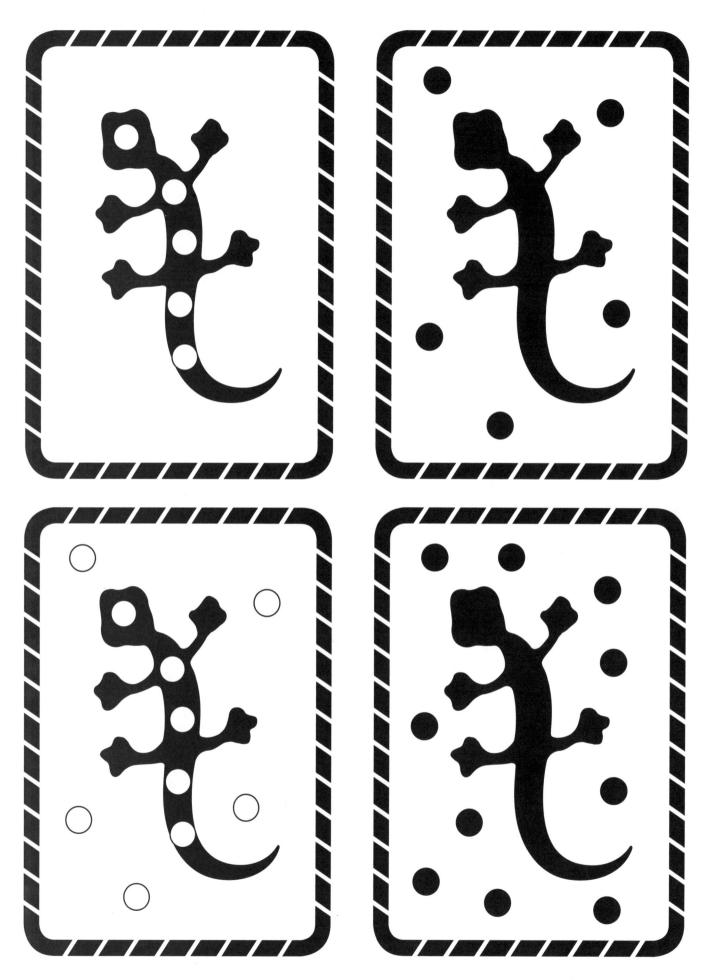

152

Idea 37
Positive Reinforcement

Using positive reinforcement is a great way to increase a desired behavior or a student's use of a skill. Students who are young or low functioning need a very basic and concrete system of reinforcement. Older students and higher functioning students can use more elaborate reinforcement systems that extend throughout the day.

Here are few guidelines.

❶ Be specific about the behavior or skill you want to increase. Pick one at a time, and specify an action verb. For example,

- Ask or gesture for help when needed.
- Work independently for 5 minutes.
- Point to the word when I say it.

❷ Use praise statements that describe the specific behavior or skill you want. For example,

- Thank you for asking for help.
- Great job working so quietly.
- Super job saying the word.

❸ Develop a concrete reinforcement system, and specify how many strips, handprints, and so on the student must receive to earn a privilege or other reinforcer. For example,

- Create a paper chain with strips of paper that you staple around each other to form links. Add a link each time you see the target behavior or skill.
- Use the student's handprint (trace them on paper or make prints using finger paint, and cut them out). Staple them together or glue them onto a piece of construction paper or poster board. Add one each time you see the target behavior or skill.
- Place a flag with the student's name at ground level against a wall. Raise it every time the student demonstrates the behavior or skill.
- Place a small plastic jar or clear container near the child. Place a bright neon Ping-Pong ball in it every time you see the behavior or skill.

153

◆ Create a menu of reinforcers and change it often. We have provided two blank menus. One has space for visuals, and the other has space for words or phrases that describe reinforcers. If you copy the menu on heavy paper and laminate it, you can change the menu daily or weekly.

◆ Make sure you and everyone else working with the student reinforces positively and consistently.

In addition to the reinforcement menus provided, there are two positive behavior contracts. The first form is designed for use with young students or those just beginning to focus on targets behaviors or skills. The second can be used with students who are being included in one or more general education class. Choose specific target behaviors or skills and fill in the forms with picture symbols, photographs, or words. Use the contract for a given amount of time to reinforce the target behaviors or skills.

Here is a list of possible reinforcers.

Materials and Activities
Hand cream
Stickers
Stamps and pads
Puzzles
Crayons
Washable markers
Video
Grab bag
Computer time
Rocking
Water play
Puppet play
Stories

Edibles
Cereals
Fruits
Juice
Pudding
Yogurt
Crackers
Vegetables

Social
Hugs
Shaking hands
High fives

Reinforcement Menu

Idea 37

Reinforcement Menu

1. _____

2. _____

3. _____

4. _____

5. _____

Idea 37

Directions for Using the Behavior Contracts

The First Form

❶ Choose one target behavior or skill and a reinforcer. Indicate the goal to students by using pictures or symbols that represent the behavior and reinforcer selected. (The example has "no hitting" as the target behavior and "listen to music" as the reinforcer.)

❷ Fill in the time intervals, circle the faces, and reinforce if the behavior has been on target.

The Second Form

❶ Select four target behaviors or skills. Write them in the boxes across the top of the form.

❷ Write the name of the class in the first column.

❸ At the bottom of the form, write the target number of yeses and the reinforcer selected by the student.

❹ Circle *Yes* if the behavior is appropriate, and *No* if not. At the end of the time interval, record the number of yeses in the box.

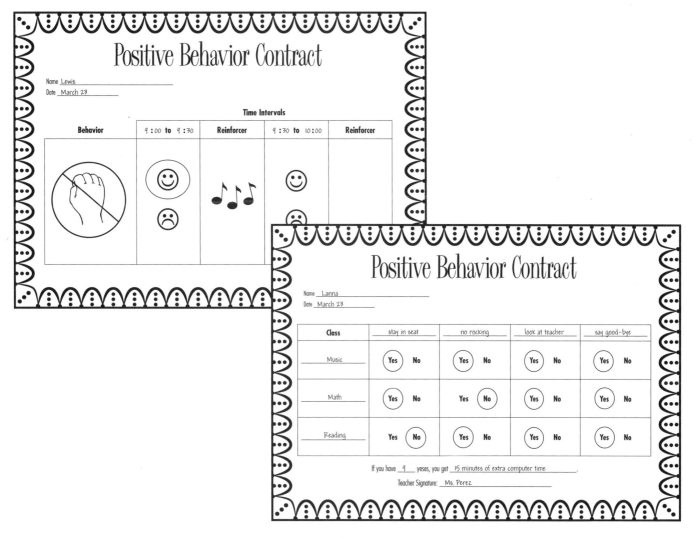

Positive Behavior Contract

Name _____

Date _____

Time Intervals

Behavior	: to :	Reinforcer	: to :	Reinforcer

Idea 37

Positive Behavior Contract

Name _____

Date _____

Class				
_____	Yes No	Yes No	Yes No	Yes No
_____	Yes No	Yes No	Yes No	Yes No
_____	Yes No	Yes No	Yes No	Yes No

If you have _____ yeses, you get _____

Teacher Signature: _____

Idea 38
What To Teach Next

Students with autism spectrum disorders vary widely in their ability to function in their social and learning environments. The scale included with this book is one method you can use to implement intervention strategies to enable them to function more effectively. The skills in our scale are directly linked to the DSM–IV–TR criteria and are broad in scope. It is also important to break skills down into more discrete tasks. For example, one item on our scale gives you information about a student's ability to use greetings or courteous phrases. However, you may want to know if there are conditions under which this same student uses speech and if so, what kind of speech. In addition, the DSM–IV–TR does not specifically address academic skills and it is important to know where to start academically for these children. The first step in determining what to teach next is to assess the student's current skills and deficiencies.

Several books provide guides that sequence academic, communication, motor, self-help, and other skills. (Two resources are listed below.) We have provided two forms; use the first one to assess the student and the second one to sequence and keep track of the skills to be taught.

⚜ Tip:

Ask parents to assess their child or adolescent at home on the same skills to determine the degree of generalization. Give parents simple ways to follow through at home with the teaching of targeted skills.

Resources

Maurice, C. (Ed.), Green, G., & Luce, S. C. (Co-Eds.) (1996). *Behavioral intervention for young children with autism.* Austin, TX: PRO-ED.

Schopler, E., Lansing, M., & Waters, L. (Eds.) (1983). *Teaching activities for autsitc children.* Austin, TX: PRO-ED.

Here's how the Assessment form works.

❶ Determine the skill area in which you want to begin, for example, communication.

❷ Choose an existing hierarchy or develop your own for that skill area and assess the child to determine mastery level. Make sure the skills you are assessing are developmentally appropriate for the student.

❸ Determine the first skill to assess from the hierarchy. Base this determination on what you already know the student can do in that skill area.

❹ Write the skill in the first box and write the observation time period in the second box on the form. Check off the settings in which the observation will occur. After observing, check the level at which the child is able to do the skill. In the last box on the form, check whether or not you are targeting that skill for intervention and write the beginning date.

Name: Martin Stevens
Date: 9-4-06

Teach Next
Assessment

Skill Areas
- ☐ academic
- ☑ communication
- ☐ imitation
- ☐ fine motor
- ☐ gross motor
- ☐ self help
- ☐ social
- ☐ other _____

Skill To Assess	Observation Time Period	Setting	Level	Target for Intervention?
Imitates two- and three-word phrases	9-4 to 9-8	☑ classroom ☑ home ☐ cafeteria ☐ play area ☐ other _____	☐ Unable to do skill ☐ Needs physical guidance ☐ Needs verbal prompting ☐ Independently demonstrates skill ☑ Generalizes skill to other settings	☑ No ☐ Yes Date to Begin _____
Requests desired items spontaneously	9-11 to 9-15	☑ classroom ☑ home ☑ cafeteria ☑ play area ☑ other _grocery store_	☐ Unable to do skill ☐ Needs physical guidance ☐ Needs verbal prompting ☑ Independently demonstrates skill ☐ Generalizes skill to other settings	☐ No ☑ Yes Date to Begin 9-18
Engages in simple exchanges of conversation	9-18 to 9-22	☑ classroom ☑ home ☐ cafeteria ☐ play area ☐ other _____	☐ Unable to do skill ☐ Needs physical guidance ☑ Needs verbal prompting ☐ Independently demonstrates skill ☐ Generalizes skill to other settings	☐ No ☑ Yes Date to Begin 10-2

Comments: ___ Martin can independently request desired items spontaneously in familiar places. However, he does not generalize to unfamiliar settings such as the store.

Teach Next
Skills Progress

Name __Martin Stevens__
Date __9-4-06__

Skill Areas

- ☐ academic
- ☑ communication
- ☐ imitation
- ☐ fine motor
- ☐ gross motor
- ☐ self help
- ☐ social
- ☐ other _____

Skill To Teach	Teaching Time Period	Setting	Materials Needed	Procedures	Level
Requests desired items spontaneously	9-18 to 9-29	☐ classroom ☐ home ☐ cafeteria ☐ play area ☑ other __store__	Auditory trainer	1. Teacher and Martin go to store to buy chips. 2. Martin enters store, teacher waits near doorway. 3. Teacher prompts as needed.	☐ Introduce ☐ Mastery ☑ Generalize
Engages in simple exchanges of conversation	10-2 to 11-2	☑ classroom ☑ home ☐ cafeteria ☐ play area ☐ other_____	Talk Prompter Cards Puppets	1. Martin and peer tutor practice using one card per week. 2. Teacher and Martin use puppets to simulate a conversation.	☑ Introduce ☐ Mastery ☐ Generalize
		☐ classroom ☐ home ☐ cafeteria ☐ play area ☐ other_____			☐ Introduce ☐ Mastery ☐ Generalize

Comments: ___Martin will first work with the Talk Prompter Cards. As he progresses, the puppets will be used for reinforcement and to promote generalization.___

Here's how the Skills Progress form works.

❶ Choose the first skill to teach from the Assessment form and write that skill in the first box and the teaching time period in the second box on the Skills Progress form. Check the settings in which the skill will be taught.

❷ Decide how you are going to teach the skill, write the materials you need, and the procedures you will use. Use one of the ideas in this book, ideas from other resources, or ideas of your own to teach the skill.

❸ Check the level to which you are teaching in the last box.

Teach Next
Assessment

Name _____

Date _____

Skill Areas

☐ academic   ☐ gross motor
☐ communication   ☐ self help
☐ imitation   ☐ social
☐ fine motor   ☐ other

Skill To Assess	Observation Time Period	Setting	Level	Target for Intervention?
_____ _____ _____	_____	☐ classroom ☐ home ☐ cafeteria ☐ play area ☐ other _____	☐ Unable to do skill ☐ Needs physical guidance ☐ Needs verbal prompting ☐ Independently demonstrates skill ☐ Generalizes skill to other settings	☐ No ☐ Yes Date to Begin _____
_____ _____ _____	_____	☐ classroom ☐ home ☐ cafeteria ☐ play area ☐ other _____	☐ Unable to do skill ☐ Needs physical guidance ☐ Needs verbal prompting ☐ Independently demonstrates skill ☐ Generalizes skill to other settings	☐ No ☐ Yes Date to Begin _____
_____ _____ _____	_____	☐ classroom ☐ home ☐ cafeteria ☐ play area ☐ other _____	☐ Unable to do skill ☐ Needs physical guidance ☐ Needs verbal prompting ☐ Independently demonstrates skill ☐ Generalizes skill to other settings	☐ No ☐ Yes Date to Begin _____

Comments: _____
_____
_____

Idea 38

Teach Next
Skills Progress

Name _____

Date _____

Skill Areas

- ☐ gross motor
- ☐ self help
- ☐ social
- ☐ other _____

- ☐ academic
- ☐ communication
- ☐ imitation
- ☐ fine motor

Skill To Teach	Teaching Time Period	Setting	Materials Needed	Procedures	Level
___ ___ ___	___	☐ classroom ☐ home ☐ cafeteria ☐ play area ☐ other ___	___ ___ ___ ___	___ ___ ___ ___	☐ Introduce ☐ Mastery ☐ Generalize
___ ___ ___	___	☐ classroom ☐ home ☐ cafeteria ☐ play area ☐ other ___	___ ___ ___ ___	___ ___ ___ ___	☐ Introduce ☐ Mastery ☐ Generalize
___ ___ ___	___	☐ classroom ☐ home ☐ cafeteria ☐ play area ☐ other ___	___ ___ ___ ___	___ ___ ___ ___	☐ Introduce ☐ Mastery ☐ Generalize

Comments: _____
_____
_____

Idea 38

Idea 39
Direct-Teach Social Skills

There are many positive social behaviors that are essential in everyday situations. Oftentimes we take for granted that students will learn these essential social skills by watching others then imitating what they do. However, a student with autism or a related disorder may not learn as incidentally or naturally as other students. Here are some social skills that you may need to teach through direct instruction, modeling, prompting, practice, and reinforcement. Whenever possible, teach these skills in the contexts in which they will be used (i.e., the locations and times they are needed as well as with the individuals who are normally present in the situations). Teaching essential skills may enable a student with autism to fit into a group, relate to peers, and avoid isolation.

Social Skills

Student __Becky Shore__ Date: Week of __November 10__

	Monday	Tuesday	Wednesday	Thursday	Friday
Social Skill	greeting others	greeting others	greeting others	greeting others	greeting others
Where To Teach	classroom	classroom	lunch room	office	classroom
Who Will Teach	Ms. Matthews	Ms. Matthews	peer tutor		
How To Teach	☐ Explanation ☑ Demonstration ☑ Teacher Modeling ☐ Peer Modeling ☐ Prompts/Cues ☐ Guided Practice ☐ Independent Practice ☐ Other_____	☐ Explanation ☐ Demonstration ☑ Teacher Modeling ☐ Peer Modeling ☐ Prompts/Cues ☑ Guided Practice ☐ Independent Practice ☐ Other_____	☐ Explanation ☐ Demonstration ☐ Teacher Modeling ☐ Peer Modeling ☑ Prompts/Cues ☐ Guided Practice ☐ Independent Practice ☑ Other _prompted to greet lunch staff_	☐ Explanation ☐ Demonstration ☐ Teacher Modeling ☐ Peer Modeling ☐ Prompts/Cues ☐ Guided Practice ☑ Independent Practice ☑ Other _will greet office staff when sent on errand_	☐ Explanation ☐ Demonstration ☐ Teacher Modeling ☐ Peer Modeling ☐ Prompts/Cues ☐ Guided Practice ☑ Independent Practice ☑ Other _will greet her parents when picked up_
Evaluation Method	☐ Trial/Response Record ☑ Observation ☐ Product/Sample ☐ Other_____	☐ Trial/Response Record ☑ Observation ☐ Product/Sample ☐ Other_____	☐ Trial/Response Record ☑ Observation ☐ Product/Sample ☐ Other_____	☐ Trial/Response Record ☑ Observation ☐ Product/Sample ☑ Other _demonstrates skill with office staff_	☑ Trial/Response Record ☑ Observation ☐ Product/Sample ☑ Other _demonstrates skill with parents_
Homework	none	practice with parents at home			Becky to record times she greets people over the weekend

167

Following are some skills (with examples) that students with autism will likely need but might not learn without being directly taught. When designing your instruction for these skills, you can use the Social Skills plan provided.

Communicating

- Asking for something (scissors for cutting)
- Asking for help (when he or she cannot reach an item)
- Greeting others (saying "hello" first)
- Joining a conversation (adding pertinent information to an ongoing discussion)
- Using courteous phrases ("please" and "thank you")

Waiting

- In line (cafeteria)
- For something to begin or end (a class activity)
- For mealtime (not snacking or starting to eat until everyone is ready)
- For help (assistance with a difficult task)
- For a turn (playing with a toy)

Transitioning

- Following a schedule independently (especially a visual or pictorial schedule not requiring verbal reminders or prompts)
- Getting ready for an activity (locating garden tools needed for planting flowers)
- Cleaning up after an activity (putting dirty dishes in the dishwasher)
- Handing in a work product when completed (turning in a finished assignment)
- Moving from one scheduled service to another (going from speech therapy to PE)

Social Skills

Student _____   Date: Week of _____

	Monday	Tuesday	Wednesday	Thursday	Friday
Social Skill					
Where To Teach					
Who Will Teach					
How To Teach	❑ Explanation ❑ Demonstration ❑ Teacher Modeling ❑ Peer Modeling ❑ Prompts/Cues ❑ Guided Practice ❑ Independent Practice ❑ Other _____	❑ Explanation ❑ Demonstration ❑ Teacher Modeling ❑ Peer Modeling ❑ Prompts/Cues ❑ Guided Practice ❑ Independent Practice ❑ Other _____	❑ Explanation ❑ Demonstration ❑ Teacher Modeling ❑ Peer Modeling ❑ Prompts/Cues ❑ Guided Practice ❑ Independent Practice ❑ Other _____	❑ Explanation ❑ Demonstration ❑ Teacher Modeling ❑ Peer Modeling ❑ Prompts/Cues ❑ Guided Practice ❑ Independent Practice ❑ Other _____	❑ Explanation ❑ Demonstration ❑ Teacher Modeling ❑ Peer Modeling ❑ Prompts/Cues ❑ Guided Practice ❑ Independent Practice ❑ Other _____
Evaluation Method	❑ Trial/Response Record ❑ Observation ❑ Product/Sample ❑ Other _____	❑ Trial/Response Record ❑ Observation ❑ Product/Sample ❑ Other _____	❑ Trial/Response Record ❑ Observation ❑ Product/Sample ❑ Other _____	❑ Trial/Response Record ❑ Observation ❑ Product/Sample ❑ Other _____	❑ Trial/Response Record ❑ Observation ❑ Product/Sample ❑ Other _____
Homework					

Idea 39

169

Idea 40
Skills Checklists

Teachers, parents, therapists, and others who work with individuals with autism often do not know where to start when teaching skills. The three skills checklists provided with this idea are useful tools when evaluating students' skills and then planning instruction. There are four levels of proficiency for each skill, ranging from "Cannot do it at all" to "Can do it without help." The information gained from completing the checklists allows adults to plan while taking into account the amount of assistance and guidance that each student requires.

When using the skills checklists, we suggest that you ask several individuals to complete the form(s) without consulting each other. After obtaining two or three evaluations, adults should meet as a team to share their impressions of the student's level of proficiency and then design relevant objectives. These checklists are not intended to replace standardized assessments but can be used effectively as informal measures of skills' mastery.

The Play Skills checklist is designed for use with young children. The Independent Living Skills checklist is intended for use with older students. Specific items from the Self-Care Skills checklist can be used with students by selecting those skills appropriate to each student's age and developmental level.

Play Skills

Skill	Cannot do it at all	Needs much help to do it	Needs little help to do it	Can do it without help
Pay attention to music				
Clap hands				
Grasp/hold large toys or objects				
Grasp/hold crayons or pencils				
Push, pull, turn toys				
Name toys and objects used for play				
Imitate gestures or movements				
Open and close lids or doors				
Name body parts				
Cut with scissors				
Paste paper or pictures				
Scribble with crayon or pencil				
Color in coloring book mostly within lines				
Do simple noninterlocking puzzles				
Do interlocking puzzles				
Play computer games				
Match colors and shapes				
Throw and catch a ball				
Kick a ball				
Hit a ball with hand(s)				
Hit a ball with a bat				
Use paints				
Use modeling clay				
Dance				
Sing				
Do simple pantomimes				
Manipulate hand puppets				
Blow bubbles				
Shovel and dump sand				
Stack blocks				
Pretend/do make believe play				
Take turns during play				

Idea 40

Self-Care Skills

Skill	Cannot do it at all	Needs much help to do it	Needs little help to do it	Can do it without help
Drink from a cup				
Eat with a spoon				
Eat with a fork				
Spread with a knie				
Cut with a knife				
Use a napkin				
Shower, bathe, and dry off				
Wash and rinse hair				
Wash face				
Wash hands				
Brush teeth				
Comb hair				
Shave (if applicable)				
Use deodorant				
Trim fingernails and toenails				
Use toilet and toilet paper				
Use tampon/sanitary napkin (if applicable)				
Select clothes that match				
Select clothes appropriate to weather				
Select clothes appropriate to social occasion				
Put dirty clothes in hamper				
Put clean clothes away				
Use washer and dryer				
Put on and take off underwear				
Put on and take off skirt/pants				
Put on and take off top/shirt				
Operate a zipper				
Button and unbutton clothes				
Fasten snaps and hooks				
Put on and take off socks				
Put on and take off shoes				
Tie shoes				
Thread and buckle belt				
Care for minor cuts				
Treat a common headache				
Treat a common nosebleed				
Use a hankerchief or tissue				

Idea 40

Independent Living Skills

Skill	Cannot do it at all	Needs much help to do it	Needs little help to do it	Can do it without help
Wash and dry dishes				
Empty trash baskets				
Sweep floor				
Mop floor				
Dust furniture				
Vacuum carpet				
Put away toys, books, clothes, etc.				
Tell basic safety fules in kitchen				
Use oven and microwave				
Identify canned or boxed foods by labels				
Use stovetop				
Get a simple snack (no cooking required)				
Make sandwich				
Fix salads/desserts				
Make cereal				
Cook a side dish or main dish				
Cook prepared foods				
Purchase groceries with a shopping list				
Find/replace foods or utensils in kitchen				
Identify/discard spoiled food				
Select foods for a well-balanced diet				
Store leftover food				
Use toaster				
Use can opener				
Use coffee maker				
Use measuring utensils				
Replace burned-out lightbulb				
Replace toilet paper roll in bathroom				
Adjust window curtains or shades				
Adjust television and radio, select stations, etc.				
Play music on CD player or radio				
Turn lights, television, etc. off when not in use				
Lock doors and windows when appropriate				
Water houseplants				
Feed, water, and clean up after pets				
Make the bed				
Change the sheets				

Idea 40

Appendix
Reproducible Icons

angry	apple	backpack	bagel
ball	banana	baseball	basketball
bathroom	book	boy	breakfast
brush	bus	cafeteria	cat
catch	cereal	chicken nuggets	chips

Appendix

coat	comb	computer	conversation
cookie	cracker	cry	cut
dinosaur	dog	doll	draw
drink	eat	excited	football
French fries	friends	frustrated	funny

Appendix

girl

glue

grapes

hamburger

happy

help

hello

home

hungry

hurt

ice cream

I don't know

juice

kick

library

listen

lunch

matching

math

me

Appendix

milk

mine

modeling clay

muffin

music

my turn

no

notebook

open

outside

paint

pants

paper

park

pencil

pizza

play

playground

popcorn

pretzel

Appendix

puppet   puzzle   quiet   raisins

read   run   sad   same

sandbox   sandwich   school   share

shirt   shoes   shorts   show me

sing   sisters   sit   skirt

Appendix

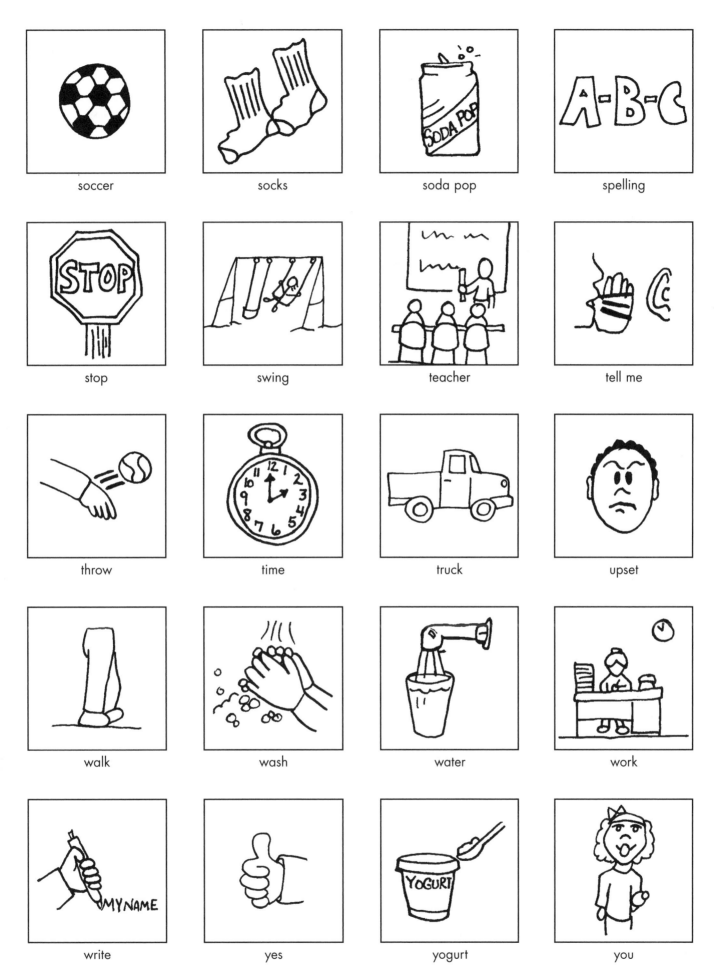

soccer	socks	soda pop	spelling
stop	swing	teacher	tell me
throw	time	truck	upset
walk	wash	water	work
write	yes	yogurt	you

Appendix